Care and Counseling
of the Aging

D0026912

Care and Counseling
of the Aging

William M. Clements

Fortress Press   Philadelphia

COPYRIGHT © 1979 BY FORTRESS PRESS

Library of Congress Cataloging in Publication Data

Clements, William M 1943-
    Care and counseling of the aging.

    (Creative pastoral care and counseling series)
    Bibliography: p.
    1. Church work with the aged. I. Title.
BV4435.C57   253.5   78-54547
ISBN 0-8006-0561-6

7120G78   Printed in the United States of America 1–561

Sally Morris Turner
1880–1967

No human being ever belongs to anyone else, and Sally Morris Turner has for eighty-one years maintained her own independence and her own individuality; we are proud of her for that. But the fact that she is a Turner pleases us too. Her having shared herself with us makes it possible for us to say that we are part of her family, and we are glad that we are.

> When Sally Morris was a girl
> She met a man named Will.
> So she became a Turner then,
> And she's a Turner still.

—Crenshaw County, Alabama
The Turner Family Reunion
1961

Contents

Series Foreword

Let me share with you some of the hopes that are in the minds of those of us who helped to develop this series—hopes that relate directly to you as the reader. It is our desire and expectation that these books will be of help to you in developing better working tools as a minister-counselor. We hope that they will do this by encouraging your own creativity in developing more effective methods and programs for helping people live life more fully. It is our intention in this series to affirm the many things you have going for you as a minister in helping troubled persons—the many assets and resources from your religious heritage, your role as the leader of a congregation, and your unique relationship to individuals and families throughout the life cycle. We hope to help you reaffirm the *power of the pastoral* by the use of fresh models and methods in your ministry.

The aim of the series is not to be comprehensive with respect to topics but rather to bring innovative approaches to some major types of counseling. Although the books are practice-oriented, they also provide a solid foundation of theological and psychological insights. They are written primarily for ministers (and those preparing for the ministry) but we hope that they will also prove useful to other counselors who are interested in the crucial role of spiritual and value issues in all helping relationships. In addition we hope that the series will be useful in seminary courses, clergy support groups, continuing education workshops, and lay befriender training.

This is a period of rich new developments in counseling and psychotherapy. The time is ripe for a flowering of creative methods and insights in pastoral care and counseling. Our expectation is that this series will stimulate grass-roots creativity as innovative methods and programs come alive for you. Some of the major thrusts that will be discussed in this series include a

new awareness of the unique contributions of the theologically
trained counselor, the liberating power of the human potentials
orientation, an appreciation of the pastoral-care function of the
ministering congregation, the importance of humanizing systems
and institutions as well as close relationships, the importance of
pastoral *care* (and not just counseling), the many opportunities
for caring ministries throughout the life cycle, the deep changes
in male-female relationships, and the new psychotherapies such
as Gestalt therapy, transactional analysis, educative counseling,
and crisis methods. Our hope is that this series will enhance your
resources for your ministry to persons by opening doorways to
understanding of these creative thrusts in pastoral care and counseling.

This volume by William Clements focuses on pastoral care
with a rapidly increasing group in our society—older persons. It
draws on the author's broad pastoral experience in working with
aging people and his depth understanding of the process of aging.
As I read the manuscript, I sensed that Bill has *been there* with
older people—in churches and in nursing homes and other institutions as well as around family tables and on park benches in the
late afternoon. I particularly appreciate his growth perspective on
aging. Bill emphasizes that each stage of the life journey holds
fresh opportunities for personal growth. He identifies those points
in the second half of life in which the tension between growth and
stagnation comes into sharp focus. His approach to aging is a
refreshing corrective to those pessimistic views that see the second half of life as a time of primary preoccupation with decline
and loss.

In this book the author integrates solid theory with the down-
to-earth realities of ministry to and with older people. He utilizes
insights from life-cycle psychology, process theology, and
psychosynthesis in a way that extends one's understanding of
creative aging and how to facilitate it. His discussion of how to
use reminiscence therapeutically is a significant contribution to
the literature on the care of older persons.

William Clements currently is assistant professor, Department
of Family Practice at the University of Iowa medical school. In
this post he has special responsibilities for teaching marriage and
family counseling skills in the residency program. His research

focus is in geriatrics and the personality problems of the aging. Prior to joining the faculty of the medical school, Bill served as Director of Pastoral Care and Counseling for the United Methodist Church in Alabama. He brings to all his professional activities the sensitivities of a warm-hearted, caring pastor.

This book will be of particular relevance to pastors who have frequent opportunities to work with older people. (I wish that my parents during their post-retirement years could have had the creative pastoral care described in these pages.) I predict that the book also will be useful to persons from a variety of other professional disciplines—nurses, physicians, family counselors, and staff members in institutions serving older people. It will be a help to family members who are struggling to relate more constructively with aging parents and other close relatives, and a valuable resource in churches and community agencies for committees on the care and continuing education of older adults.

One theme of this book touched me with special power—Bill's emphasis on the importance of getting in touch with our feelings about our own aging. I hope you'll try the experiential exercises described toward the close of chapter 1. As the author makes clear, awareness of our attitudes and feelings about our own aging constitutes an essential foundation for growth-enabling approaches to aging persons. I'm pleased to commend this book to you for both your personal and professional growth.

HOWARD J. CLINEBELL, JR.

Preface

In the preparation and writing of this book I was reminded of the many people who have contributed to my life journey. Some of the most significant persons appear in the pages of this book as live illustrations from my pastoral experience. All names have been changed of course and fictitious identities have been constructed to insure the privacy of those who appear.

Several other people have been significant in my personal and professional development as well. Roy Woodruff and Tom Kennedy helped me learn about myself in the midst of ministries with elderly people. Allen Moore of Claremont was a rare teacher who provided wise counsel and generous support for my budding research interests in an infrequently traveled area—personality and religion among elderly people. The Chairman of the Department of Family Practice here at the University of Iowa also deserves special mention: Robert E. Rakel was not only generous in allowing sufficient time away from regular responsibilities so that this work could proceed at an adequate pace, but in many other ways as well he has made it possible for me to develop my ministry of counseling, teaching, and research. Claudia Richards and Kim Koeppen patiently typed and retyped the manuscript; it is a pleasure to work with them.

Howard Clinebell first invited my participation in the Creative Pastoral Care and Counseling Series when I was the Director of Pastoral Care and Counseling for the United Methodist Church in Alabama. Later, when on the faculty here at Iowa, work began in earnest on this book. Throughout the months of writing, the editors have been most helpful to me, particularly following a significant health crisis when Howard Stone and Howard Clinebell each reached out and sensitively touched my life. For me they have embodied what this series is all about.

Betty Clements has been closely involved in all aspects of the preparation of this book. Beyond helping to edit the manuscript in its preliminary form, she arranged the mass of material I had collected for the last chapter into a recognizable whole and skillfully annotated the contents. Both her encouragement and skill have improved the book.

It is my hope that you will find the reading of *Care and Counseling of the Aging* to be a stimulus for your ministry. If at the conclusion of the final chapter you initiate one innovative program or assist through counseling someone who would not otherwise have been helped, then you will have fulfilled one of the dreams behind this book. It is also my hope that you gain an increased sense of meaning and value from your regular pastoral activities with elderly people—preaching and visitation continue as the mainstay. I believe that your ministry does make a difference in the lives of those persons with whom you have contact, particularly the aging. Good luck in your venture!

1. Getting in Touch with Aging

It was a typical Sunday morning for four young seminarians—
hurried "breakfast" of almost stale sweet rolls and strong coffee
consumed on a railroad platform in the crisp coolness of early
fall. When the train arrived at the station each of us silently took a
seat in the same car and began studying for the big examination
on Monday. As the train pulled away, one of the clergy-to-be was
already trying to scribble notes on a pad precariously balanced on
one knee while the coach gently swayed back and forth.

Slowly the train made its way up the banks of the Hudson
River past majestic bluffs glowing with the beautiful colors of
fall. For forty minutes we scarcely looked up from our work—we
could just as well have been in a tunnel under Manhattan—until
we arrived in Tarrytown. Then the books were packed away and
as we walked up the hill leading to the church conversation
began—friendly jokes mixed in with a discussion of lesson plans
for Sunday school.

Following classes and worship we met together again, according to custom, to drive home with one of the church families for
dinner. So far it had been a rather typical day in the field work
situation.

Entering our hosts' home, we could smell a delicious aroma of
roast beef baking in the oven. Today we were eating with an
unusual family: Mr. and Mrs. Wilson, Bobby, Jenny, and Mr.
Wilson's grandfather, who was a part of the family and lived in
the home. As we stood around the table hungrily eyeing the beef,
I wondered who would be asked to give the blessing. Mr. Wilson
asked Grandpa, who, standing with a cane in both hands to support his frail body, deftly cut through the generations with a
prayer which has stuck in my memory to this day: "O Lord, we
pray that the cares and demands of education will not blind the
eyes of our guests to the beauty of this life and the love of our

fellowship. May this meal be a blessing in our lives. Amen.''
And it was.

Over the years I have thought lovingly of Grandpa Wilson and
his guests that Sunday morning. Perhaps this event affected me so
deeply because I simply didn't expect such sensitive insight from
a man born shortly after the Civil War, a centenarian who walked
with great difficulty and wore two hearing aids. Grandpa brings
to my mind Rabbi Ben Ezra, in Robert Browning's poem:

I

Grow old along with me!
The best is yet to be,
The last of life, for which the first was made:
Our times are in His hand
Who saith "A whole I planned,
Youth shows but half; trust God: see all nor be afraid!''

VII

For thence, —a paradox
Which comforts while it mocks, —
Shall life succeed in that it seems to fail:
What I aspired to be,
And was not, comforts me.
A brute I might have been, but would not sink i' the scale.

XV

Youth ended, I shall try
My gain or loss thereby;
Leave the fire ashes, what survives is gold:
And I shall weigh the same,
Give life its praise or blame:
Young, all lay in dispute; I shall know, being old.

XVII

So still within this life,
Though lifted o'er its strife,
Let me discern, compare, pronounce at last,
"This rage was right i' the main,
That acquiescence vain:
The Future I may face now I have proved the Past.''

XXXII

So, take and use thy work:
Amend what flaws may lurk,
What strain o' the stuff, what warpings past the aim!
My times be in Thy hand!
Perfect the cup as planned!
Let age approve of youth, and death complete the same!*

Probably all of us possess cherished memories of an aged person who has meant a great deal to us at a particular moment in our pilgrimage through life. Outside of my own grandmother, Grandpa Wilson was probably the first older person I had really known—or allowed to know me. I had seen a lot of old people before but only from a distance; I had not felt such strong identification with them.

As it was, I became aware of a truly novel idea: I am growing old! Perhaps without such an overwhelmingly positive encounter with Grandpa Wilson I could have denied the obvious reality of my own aging for decades yet. With massive cultural support from a society which discourages acceptance of aging, who knows, I might have been seventy before I admitted such an obvious and basic fact about myself!

Now, however, I had come alive to the personal knowledge that I, like all of creation, was growing old. This awareness brought ambivalent feelings about my own aging to the surface—and does to this day. At times it seems easy to accept and even rejoice in the fact that I may grow old like Grandpa Wilson. At other moments I feel myself recoiling in horror at the thought that my aging could possibly flow in a different direction, leading instead to a helpless or utterly senile condition.

Ambivalence about Aging

When society does admit the existence of the aged, the admission is all too often accompanied by decidedly negative overtones. We think immediately of dreary nursing homes filled with helpless, senile caricatures of human beings. Ministers at times may see the positive side of the nursing home as well, but if you are like me you will have found yourself saddened more than once by the helplessness, and especially the assumptions of helplessness, you encounter there.

Walking down the wide corridor to Lucy's room and discreetly observing as much as possible of my new surroundings in the nursing home, I tried to listen to the nurse describe the patient I was about to see for the first time. A few residents looked up from their TV programs and waved to us as we passed. One woman sat comfortably by the window in her room happily crocheting. Another shuffled slowly toward us, holding the safety bannister for security. The nurse reported that Lucy, in her late eighties, had begun to change about a month ago—becoming more distant, less cooperative, and tearful.

When we reached Lucy's room we found her lying in bed on her back, fully dressed, and staring at the ceiling. As the nurse introduced me, Lucy glanced in my direction and then without a word promptly reached for a towel and draped it over her face. She lay very still, and with head covered looked almost like a corpse. The only sound in the room came from the TV sets at the other end of the hall—a faint background noise in the distance. Lucy remained mute. I attempted to engage her in conversation a time or two but without success.

Finally the nurse left, indicating that she had to go about her duties elsewhere. Almost as soon as the door clicked shut Lucy removed the towel from her face—she was ready to talk. For the next hour or so we had an intense and moving encounter. It became obvious that throughout her life Lucy had maintained a great ability to care for herself and make her own decisions. Even after twenty years of retirement she was still paying her own way in the nursing home and felt relatively secure. She had always been "intentional" about her life, choosing the best of the various options of which she was aware.

In spite of the good things Lucy told me about her past, her obvious sadness filled the room. She detailed how with advancing age she had gradually found it necessary to give up a little more autonomy here and a little more independence there until a few years ago when she had decided to enter the nursing home. Even this decision was not a blow to her self-esteem, however, because *she* had made it. Besides, there were still options open to her here at the home, such as how to decorate her room and which activities to pursue. But listening to her talk I knew that something was radically wrong, and it was something we hadn't yet mentioned. I reached out to hold her hand: "Lucy, do things seem sort of hopeless for you?" Slowly the tears flowed down her cheeks as she looked at me and nodded her head. Her deep sobbing said to me, "You can never know how hopeless I feel." Gradually words began to emerge, half-coherent because of her emotions, and I thought I heard her say, "They keep putting syrup on my cornbread, and I have asked them so many times not to do that, but it is still there every night."

What that meant for this woman in her eighties bolted into my awareness like a freight train! Lucy, who had been able to make major decisions all her life, now was not allowed even to decide what went in her own mouth! How much more could her decisional environment shrink? No wonder Lucy was feeling helpless, angry, ineffective. In the face of such present reality she was now effectively making her last decision—to die.

To me, Lucy's condition even exceeded in pathos the picture of old age we see in Ecclesiastes:

> And remember your creator in the days of your youth, before evil days come and the years approach when you say, 'These give me no pleasure', before sun and light and moon and stars grow dark, and the clouds return after the rain;
>
> > the day when those who keep the house tremble
> > and strong men are bowed;
> > when the women grind no longer at the mill,
> > because day is darkening at the windows
> > and the street doors are shut;
> > when the sound of the mill is faint,
> > when the voice of the bird is silenced,
> > and song notes are stilled,
> > when to go uphill is an ordeal
> > and a walk is something to dread.
>
> > Yet the almond tree is in flower,
> > the grasshopper is heavy with food
> > and the caper bush bears its fruit,
>
> while man goes to his everlasting home. And the mourners are already walking to and fro in the street
>
> > before the silver cord has snapped,
> > or the golden lamp been broken,
> > or the pitcher shattered at the spring,
> > or the pulley cracked at the well,
>
> or before the dust returns to the earth as it once came from it, and the breath to God who gave it.*

The truth of course is that most aged people are neither so radically perceptive nor so utterly helpless as my memory images of Grandpa Wilson and Lucy, but somehow the rational knowledge that I probably won't be like either has done little or nothing to abolish my ambivalent feelings. Along with all of life, we are all participants in an inexorable process of creation, growth, and death. In order to grow emotionally and spiritually we have to age, because to grow is to age and to age is to grow. Between creation and death is growth, and when growth stops death begins. I find myself both attracted and repulsed at the thought of being involved in life with absolutely no guarantee that my old age will be a time of synthesis and putting things in order.

My silent inner dialogue between faith and despair is heightened in the midst of a ministry with old persons. Cognitively I know that God's redeeming love encompasses each of us regardless of our condition, and yet I feel at times as if this were not so—as if becoming aged makes me unacceptable, as if ultimate acceptance in an ontological sense depends on the maintenance of a high level of mental and physical functioning. As painful as it is for me to admit, I fear that my practice of ministry has often been guided more by this feeling than by my belief in God's all-encompassing love, which does not require of us certain abilities nor value us more highly at certain ages than at others.

This dichotomy between belief and feeling, which clearly affects the ordering of my pastoral priorities, is strengthened by the absence of an adequately developed theology of aging to undergird the practice of ministry. As religious communities we have failed to relate our reflections about aging to the substance of our faith.

This chasm within our theological traditions has its parallel also in secular society where we have both neglected the study of aging (gerontology) and institutionalized our disregard for aging persons. What is it within us as individuals and as a society that contributes to this condition of neglect?

Psychological Blocks

The theological gap and societal deficit may derive from certain psychological blocks. Through modern psychology and sociology we can now discover these obstacles and describe them; the inhibiting forces can be understood and examined. As a result of such discovery and learning, the natural flow of our energy and thought can be restored. We can become aware of our own aging, and consequently cease to neglect the old persons within the sphere of our pastoral responsibility.

These forces which shape our attitudes toward aging are not of volcanic intensity, erupting in any moment and compelling us to behave in certain ways. Rather they possess only static energy, such as that created by a large earthen dam which blocks a stream to form a lake. The water pressing against the dam possesses enormous energy, but this energy does not normally force the dam to do something; it is just there, the natural flow of water blocked by the dam.

Repression

The psychological equivalent of an earthen dam is repression. Repression is a powerful force that tends to block our awareness of certain thoughts and feelings. Any thought or mental image which seems to make us more anxious tends to become repressed. As a result we simply are not aware of those anxiety-provoking ideas and situations; we avoid thinking or doing anything which might bring them into our field of awareness; we do not even realize there is a problem.

If our inner images of being aged cause us to become anxious we simply curtail the awareness of our own aging. For instance, we may watch our children grow up year by year, and yet think of ourselves as always the same age. If visiting in a nursing home makes us ill at ease we may tend to forget that we haven't called there in several weeks—or months.

Repression is the psychological mechanism which enables us to avoid undue anxiety. But there is a price to be paid for this comfort, as Seward Hiltner has suggested:

> I have become even more convinced in recent years that the tendency to deny, evade, or otherwise fail to take seriously the confrontation of the aging process (before either person or group reaches what is currently defined as older years) is either first or second on the list of "repressed" but vital concerns in our present culture. . . . One incidental result of this repression is that there are, in an important sense, no experts on aging.*

The church, one institution in our society with a high percentage of aged and aging members, has a great opportunity to think and minister creatively, but the repression of our own aging must be lifted if we are to become sufficiently comfortable and anxiety-free for our normal creative processes to flow.

Selective Inattention

The church can also block awareness of our responsibility to the aged through selective inattention. We see this particular defense mechanism at work both individually and collectively:

The "lay visitors" program at St. Stephen's Church seemed to be getting off to a good start. The planning meetings had been well attended and all lay visitors seemed to have understood their roles and objectives through a process of group discussion and presentations by the pastor. Each person had participated in at least two role plays which were designed to facilitate learning and calm initial anxieties. The objectives of the visitation program were twofold: evangelism and pastoral care through a home visitation program. The evangelism effort was to be concerned with a new housing development which was opening on the edge of town, populated by young families moving in to enjoy the small-town atmosphere while working in a larger city a few minutes away. The pastoral-care emphasis was to be with persons from within the fellowship of the church who because of unusual life circumstances, such as bereavement or illness, were felt to be especially receptive to caring visitors. Of course St. Stephen's had its share of shut-ins who no longer made it to worship services but continued to support the church spiritually and financially. However, the parish also contained several aged dynamos, one of whom had just completed a term as mayor after his "retirement" several years previously, and another of whom was a sought-after substitute teacher despite her advancing years. Neither of these had been recruited for the planning committee or asked to serve as lay visitors. Of course neither of them would complain, because their lives had always been meaningful and would continue to be.

Like repression, selective inattention can also protect us from the anxiety associated with a sense of our own finitude. It enables us automatically to select and organize our perceptions into a meaningful picture or image.

Actually selective inattention is also a necessary protection against the kind of information overload which might overwhelm us. We simply can't be aware of everything at the same time. For example, we may notice the information in an advertisement but be unable to remember the pictures, or vice versa.

In ministry also it is quite natural for us to be most keenly aware of or attend most diligently to those ideas and persons which seem to have the most meaning for us at any one moment in time. Because of this psychological phenomenon the aged are often seen and yet not seen. We are aware of them within our midst but may not, for example, fully utilize this awareness when planning activities or recruiting lay workers for a new thrust in the congregation's ministry. Since, in our society at least, the elderly are not frequently thought of as active bearers of ministry, we often deprive ourselves of their significant help and advice because of our selective inattention.

Getting in Touch with Your Aging

If we can identify and deal with the psychological blocks and come to terms with our own aging, we can narrow the chasm separating "them" from "me." As you work through the following exercises I hope some images and thoughts relating to your own aging will emerge in your consciousness. If we can allow such images and half-forgotten feelings to emerge, and even engage them in dialogue, we can more easily accept them as parts of ourselves and in them discover an important creative impulse.

Before you begin the first exercise* find a place and a time when you can be alone without distractions for about thirty minutes. You will need paper and pen in order to record your experiences.

Exercise 1: The Old Person

1. Find an undisturbed place, set aside some time, sit back and relax! Allow your feet and leg muscles to relax. Experience the sensations of your body becoming loose and comfortable. Take a few moments to loosen other muscles, becoming progressively aware of your sense of well-being. Now take a few deep breaths, exhaling slowly. When you are ready you may proceed to the next step in a spirit of relaxed expectancy.

2. In your imagination picture yourself in a room alone. (Most people find it helpful to proceed with their eyes closed once the directions for each step are clear.) Allow yourself to experience aloneness in your room.

3. Over in the corner you notice a large door. Move over to it. Begin to notice its size, construction, color, hinges, and latch. Above the door there appears a sign which reads "Old People."
4. Open the door and allow a few of the old people beyond it to enter the room with you. Move about and notice what you see and hear. Don't interrupt. Just observe, noticing anything that seems particularly to draw your interest.
5. Pick out the individual most interesting to you and see if you can begin to relate in some way. Don't rush. Reciprocity will develop in its own time.
6. Get a clearer picture of the old person in your mind. Begin to ask some questions. Listen attentively for the answers. Ask what your old person wants. Make a mental note. Ask why. Ask what the person needs. Again make a mental note. Ask why again.
7. Imagine yourself becoming this old person. *Be* the old person, identifying completely with your image. What does the world look like to you now? How do you experience your environment? What would your life be like if you *remained* this old person?
8. Become yourself again. How do you feel about this old person? Talk it over with that person. Listen for the dialogue, making mental note of anything which seems significant.
9. You and the old person are now outside in the warm sunshine. You have a sense that you and the old person are being enveloped in a creative atmosphere. Something is going to happen, perhaps between the two of you, perhaps to you alone. Things will be different. Talk with the old person about this change or difference. How might your life be different?
10. Say good-bye to your old person. Make a mental note of your feelings now that you have parted company.
11. Allow yourself to come back into the here and now. Take in hand your paper and pen, writing as fully as possible whatever is important to you. You may describe the total experience, or write about an important moment of dialogue.

Whatever seems most significant is the point of your beginning.

After you have finished this first exercise you may need to take a break. It's better to be relaxed and comfortable at a later session than to plunge ahead if your schedule is nagging you or you are tired. Besides, it sometimes helps to let an exercise "percolate" for awhile.

Now that you have completed the exercise of imagining an old person, talking with this person, and writing a description of your experience, I hope you have developed a heightened sense of the powerful role that repression plays in your life. Many people are a bit surprised to discover a figure like their old person—a person who has great personal significance, yet has never before been thought of so directly nor experienced so immediately. From time to time some people have found it helpful to reengage their old person in dialogue, nourishing and replenishing those growthful sparks which seem to emerge from such encounters. You might experiment with this too in a process of further discovery leading to a larger synthesis of those images which relate to your aging.

Exercise 2: The Sealed Letter

Again make sure that you have at least twenty minutes alone in a place where you will be undisturbed. Since this exercise involves writing yourself a letter, you will want to have paper, pen, and a writing table available.

1. Develop a mental image of what you will be like when you retire. Your image may have visual, cognitive, and emotional elements. Be sensitive to these and any other factors which seem to be present. Let your image be what it wants to be, not what you want it to be.
2. Take your time in considering these questions: How old will you be when you retire? From today how far off is your retirement? Where would you like to be living then? What sorts of things might you be doing? How might your personality have developed by then? What obstacles will you have overcome? What present-day problems might have become

    transformed into things that are a meaningful part of your life
and don't have to be changed?

3. Let your awareness begin to focus on a letter which you are to
   open when you retire, a letter written some time ago. In this
   letter you may find valuable advice, support, caution, or help.
   Develop a sense of this letter before you.
4. Imagine that *today* you have retired and the letter has just been
   delivered to you.
5. What would you want it to say? Why? What constructive
   input might it contain?
6. Now begin to write yourself this letter. Put down on paper
   whatever needs to be said. Take your time, allowing your
   creative energy free reign to express itself in the letter. (If you
   are already a retiree write a letter that *would* have made a
   difference had it been available.)
7. What are you aware of about yourself now that you have
   completed the exercise? How might this make a difference to
   you in the way you live your life and relate to yourself and
   other people?

    All of us can assent to the notion that with a little luck we will
someday retire. Yet this knowledge does not seem to play a very
large part in our planning for the future. In the younger years
retirement is perhaps nothing more than a vague sense of something out of view over the horizon. In the middle years it is easy
to delude ourselves with the idea that we are too busy to deal with
it creatively. Then one day that far distant horizon is no longer
"someday" or even "next year" but is much more immediate,
and the question of what life holds in store for us and whether
there will ever be enough time and money "to do all the things
we always wanted to do" is no longer academic. If you choose to
let it, your sealed letter can be a first step in opening up the
possibility of your planning and constructively shaping what retirement can be like for you in advance of its actual occurrence.

Societal Stereotyping

    While repression and selective inattention are most frequently
associated with the psychological functioning of individuals, they

also occur in society at large. In the constant reshuffling of issues which we as a society (and church) choose to address, the aged seem to end up further down the list of priorities than either their sheer numbers or their needs would appear to warrant. As churches (and legislatures) we simply do not think of aging and the aged sufficiently often or intently to alter substantially those priorities which have always seemed to guide our decisions.

Beyond reflecting collectively the repression and selective inattention of our individual psyches society, like the individuals within it, also has a tendency to stereotype persons according to age. Such stereotyping limits our capacity to perceive aged people accurately and cripples our efforts to minister to them creatively. Ageism, like sexism and racism, is a form of prejudice which deludes us into thinking we know more than we actually do about the wants and needs of a certain group. We then disregard contradictory information as indicating an exception or an accident rather than as feedback which should cause us to examine our basic assumptions.

Sometimes persons who have themselves been discriminated against unwittingly participate in perpetuating the myths and half-truths about growing old. Even where one's personal experience contradicts the stereotype ("I am enjoying myself more now than when I was younger") the older person is likely to assume that it still applies to others ("Being old is really awful for all those poor souls").

Some years ago I remember being repeatedly surprised at the vitality and healthy adjustment of many aged persons within my care. To discover that Mr. Green, who was in his mid-seventies, enjoyed bowling twice a week simply astonished me. Undoubtedly I had shared an internalized yet unacknowledged stereotype whereby aged people are usually thought to be disabled and unhappy. Hence my surprise when experiences turned out differently from what I had expected.

Exercise 3: Stereotypical Phrases

To help identify the stereotypes (both positive and negative) present in your mind this simple exercise may prove useful. You will need pen and paper.

1. Quickly and without analysis or censorship jot down those words or phrases which flow into your consciousness when you think of old people. Do not pause to think about them or wonder about their accuracy. Stop only when you have filled a page or when your mind seems completely empty.
2. Now, without pausing for reflection, quickly jot down on another sheet those words or phrases which describe activities in which old people spend a lot of time.

After you have completed both lists think for awhile about what you have written. Think too of specific old people you know. How well do they fit your stereotype? Does your special old person from Exercise 1 fit your stereotype or represent an exception to the rule?

You might also find it interesting to compare your lists with the graphs in Appendix A at the back of this book. These four graphs present a few highlights from an important national survey commissioned by the National Council on Aging in which a selected cross section of over four thousand adults in the age groups eighteen to sixty-four and sixty-five or older were given in-depth interviews by Louis Harris and Associates.* The study sought "to increase our understanding of aging and to document both the image and reality of old age in the United States."

Are the words and phrases you jotted down more like those of the younger or the older respondents in the Harris survey? Do your lists support the societal stereotypes or contradict them? Why?

Consider for a moment how your phrases intersect with your ministry. Do you see correspondences between your images of older persons and your pastoral engagement with them? What might your ministry to the aging be like if your phrases were more like those of the sixty-five-and-older respondents?

Professional Development and Personal Growth

Personal functioning and growth, for most of us, do not occur in isolation from professional development and skills; indeed the two are closely intertwined. How I think of myself and my old age has significance not only for the directions my life will take personally but also for my spiritual and professional role as pastor. The more I become aware of my own aging as a present reality which extends into the future, the more sensitive I become to persons around me whose spiritual and emotional needs in some way relate to their process of aging. Thus the movement from a personal, introspective discovery about my own aging gains a social dimension as it becomes translated into an added sensitivity for ministry.

2. Time and the Illusion of Age

All the world's a stage, and all the men and women merely players. They have their exits and entrances; and one man in his time plays many parts, his acts being seven ages. At first, the infant mewling and puking in the nurse's arms. And then the whining school-boy, with his satchel and shining morning face, creeping like a snail unwillingly to school. And then the lover, sighing like furnace, with a woeful ballad made to his mistress' eyebrow. Then a soldier, full of strange oaths, and bearded like the pard; jealous in honour, sudden and quick in quarrel, seeking the bubble reputation even in the cannon's mouth. And then the justice, in fair round belly with good capon lines, with eyes severe and beard of formal cut, full of wise saws and modern instances; and so he plays his part. The sixth age shifts into the lean and slipper'd pantaloon, with spectacles on nose and pouch on side; his youthful hose, well saved, a world too wide for his shrunk shank; and his big manly voice, turning again toward childish treble, pipes and whistles in his sound. Last scene of all, that ends this strange eventful history, is second childishness, and mere oblivion, sans teeth, sans eyes, sans taste, sans everything.
　　　　　　　　　—William Shakespeare, *As You Like It*

Shakespeare does it again! Here we see clearly a reflection of our dominant Western image of the human life cycle—from the "mewling and puking" of infancy to the "sans everything" of old age. Our model for aging in the first half of life seems to involve growth and ascendancy, for the last half of life decline and deterioration. Thus for many persons in our society being old is identified with physical loss and the process of becoming forgotten by the world around.

The Low-High-Low Sequence

Undoubtedly such an archetype of the life-span does communicate truth—for who among us has not known the helplessness which characterizes infancy and the period preceding natural death? Our natural perspective on life is from a vantage point centered in the mid-years, with a commanding view of the generations on each side.

On the one hand we believe that we can see clearly the process by which persons move from infancy through childhood and adolescence into adulthood. Maturational changes, while often dramatic, occur in a regular, almost predictable sequence, with physical growth providing an outward and visible manifestation of a concurrent inward process of emotional and spiritual development.

On the other hand, when we shift our gaze in the opposite direction, we also observe and experience that as adults we age and grow old. The first sign we may notice is that we are "chuffing" a bit as we climb familiar steps, but since our lives do not depend on physical prowess for survival we do not feel unduly threatened or even limited by the normal course of physical aging. Extending our vision even further down the path of life, however, we cannot fail to notice that some persons as they progress into old age eventually become quite feeble in body or mind.

Mid-life seems to be an elevated position toward which the youth develop and from which the aged decline. Life seems to be a progression from a low in the early years to a high in middle age, and thereafter declining to another low in old age. Our mid-years perspective suggests that life for most people occurs in a low-high-low sequence, with middle age as the peak and childhood and old age as surrounding valleys.

A similar perspective applies to other areas of life as well. The life cycle of the family, considered from the standpoint of childbearing and child-rearing, shows the same coalescing, expanding, and contracting pattern. An individual's lifetime earnings follow the same low-high-low sequential development, increasing during the early years of employment and declining at retirement.

The temptation is to assume that the low-high-low model fits all of life and thereby expresses an immutable, fundamental truth about being human. Paul W. Pruyser suggests to the contrary that our tendency to view life as shaped by the low-high-low pattern is an illusion which blinds us to alternative views of reality. "So much in the world proclaims a tripartite or triphrasic pattern with a dominant center that we come to think of this pattern as a cosmic, ordained reality, and as a leitmotiv of life.''*

Pruyser is correct. The low-high-low scheme of viewing developmental reality is an illusion. Grounded in the obvious fact of physical ascendancy followed by decline, it neglects or misinterprets other forms of experience and existence, and hence *appears* to communicate more about the human condition than it acutally does.

Not only does the illusion fail to deal adequately with the diverse elements which constitute human existence (such as emotion and will); it also fails to account sufficiently for human wholeness, which is never "a mere composite of separate faculties."† Within the low-high-low pattern wholeness seems all too closely identified with physical health and functioning. Aging is then likely to be viewed as the organism's attempt to deal with a series of irreversible physical losses (or other symbolic losses) instead of a time in which the person continues the lifelong challenge between growth and stagnation, between realizing ever new possibilities and the mere repetition of an earlier history.

Meaning and the Perspective on Time

In our modern Western society the attainment of fourscore and seven years is no longer likely to be considered an accomplishment in itself. Old age is viewed less and less as a meaningful reward for life well lived, and more and more as a "question" to be faced: "Who am I? What is the meaning of my life?" While such a question may seem to pose the classic problem of identity confronted also in the earlier decades of life, the context in which it now arises is significantly different. The older person, having spent more time in the process of living, has accumulated a rich diversity of life experiences along the way, so that the entire complex of historical and environmental conditions within which the question is asked has changed. This new context often leads to novel perspectives on life issues and to a transformation of earlier answers into a fabric of meaning that is unique to old age.

One important factor which contributes to the creation of this new context for the existential question of meaning is the individual's perspective on time. The concept of "life-time" as an entity stretching from date of birth until moment of death is one which persons seem to develop fairly early in the life process. Each of us gradually acquires a sense of where we fall on this continuum of time within the human life cycle.

The teenager deals with the question of personal meaning from a perspective in which the birth-time is relatively close and the time of death quite distant—so far away in fact that it is almost lost from view. For youth personal time is likely to seem almost limitless, supporting dreams of virtual immortality with an endless future holding the promise of innumerable possibilities for growth and personal development.

In middle age most people experience a change in their perspective on time. Until this point in life one's sense of personal place on the life-time continuum derived mainly from proximity to the time of birth, with attention focused on the interval between birth and the present (middle age) and on all that one has accomplished since the days of childhood. Now, however, the interval perceived most acutely becomes that of time remaining instead of time elapsed. Instead of a limitless future with innumerable options, the middle-aged person experiences a finite future with the possibility of choosing from among the available options those which best actualize the values and personal preferences formed in the first half of life. One senses that life does not continue forever; the future has an end point, even though it may be decades away. Much of the restlessness of middle age seems to stem from this change in the experience of life-time.

Early old age likewise has its own sense of time, involving a long interval of past time and an uncertain future with no assurance of decades to follow. The person senses that it is too late to change directions because not enough time remains to start again. Early old age becomes a period of "catching up," in which recapitulation of one's personal history—reminiscence—plays a major role. Since time no longer stretches endlessly forward over the horizon, the mind reaches back over the decades as past memories become more prominent in current daily life and earlier moments are recalled, reexamined, and reexperienced.

The existential question of meaning has a slightly different flavor too, being posed in the past tense as the person moves through early old age. Instead of the youthful "Who am I becoming?" or the middle-aged "Who am I?" and "Do I want to remain this person for the time I have left?" the person now asks "Who have I been?" and "What has been the meaning of my life?" Thus in early old age the present moment is given significance by its relationship to the past.

Old age is a difficult period of life for the rest of us to comprehend, not only because it is a distinctive stage in the life cycle but also because it has a different perspective on its place within the life-time continuum. Normally, without reflection, most of us , experience time in terms of a past-present-future sequence, and such an understanding serves us well in our everyday lives. We assume a succession of moments in which the previous moment is now past, the succeeding moment is future, and the current moment is experienced as present time. We routinely operate on the basis of such an understanding of linear time as moving from past to present to future.

As we have seen, however, each age of life experiences time somewhat differently. When we think about the human life cycle from the inside as a person doing the experiencing—rather than from the outside as an objective observer—we discover that youth tend to be more future-oriented, middle-agers with their concern for productivity tend to be more oriented to the present, and those in early old age experience, through reminiscence, more of the past. So from the perspective of the actual participants in the life cycle, as we move from youth to old age the relative emphasis accorded time moves from the future to the present and then to the past. From a developmental standpoint the usual chronological progression from past to present to future is thus exactly reversed in the movement toward old age: instead of a grammatical past-present-future sequence the existential focus is on future-present-past. This interesting reversal is significant for an understanding of the aging process.

Directivity and Creativity in the *Now*

Old age is uniquely oriented to the *now*. Its sense of *nowness* is different from the sense of time in youth, middle age, and early old age. Because there is no promise of years yet to be lived, the future does not have the power to justify the present moment, as in youth or middle age. Neither does the past justify the present, as in early old age, when to have been someone gave meaning to the present. The sense of *now* in old age does not need some extrinsic reason for existence either in society or in the human life cycle. It can afford contentment in its own right—which for the rest of us can make it a stumbling block to our comprehension of the meaningfulness of old age.

The low-high-low pattern of human development and the unique perspective on time in old age—the sense of *now*—together wreak havoc with our usual understanding of directivity. Normally we think of directivity in the younger years as movement toward some distant future goal. Steps taken in the direction of this goal are considered meaningful activity. Though any one day's progress toward the goal may appear minuscule when compared to the distance yet to be covered, there remains a sense of directivity in which the person is reaching out for what is not yet, lured on by the hint of what could be.

For old age, however, the future holds no such enticement to risk all in a leap of faith into the unknown, an exchange of certainty for uncertain possibility. There is no remoteness to the future as in the days of youth, nor is the present moment packed with productivity as in the middle years, and for the most part the "catching up" has all been done in early old age. What is most real is *now*.

Society offers little understanding of or support for this sense of *now* in old age. It simply does not recognize the aged as possessing the quality of directivity with a positive sense of movement toward significant goals. As a result younger persons do not move through life with high expectations for old age luring them toward fulfillment, nor do middle-aged persons long for aspects of old age with the same intensity that children long for the prerogatives and responsibilities of adulthood.

What the younger generations lack is a basic understanding of the means by which creativity becomes actualized or incarnate in the *now* of old age. If the movement implied in directivity is sensed only when there is a *distant* future, then perhaps there is indeed "no life after high school." In fact, however, the distance to the future becomes progressively shorter with each succeeding moment which moves any person one microsecond closer to the ultimate goal. When young people emphasize the eventual end point, the goal toward which all effort is directed, then growth is in danger of being experienced solely as a means of "getting where you want to go," and the creative moment—that gap between the present and the future in which creativity becomes incarnate—loses its meaning except insofar as it furthers the impetus toward goal-directed behavior.

Likewise in middle age the creative moment is in danger of being swallowed up by a supposedly greater value, that of present productivity. Creative moments which lead to tangible productivity are experienced and rewarded in middle age as worthful, but creativity which cannot be translated into palpable material objects is not. Growth is experienced only in terms of productive results which the world can see and respond to positively.

Early old age and old age itself, however, have their creative moments—still there in the gap between the present and the future—even if they are not as likely to be experienced in their subservience to goal-directed behavior or to productivity as in previous decades. Instead, early old age experiences creativity in the directivity which synthesizes the past, and old age experiences it in the context of the *now*. In both cases creativity and growth lose some of their relative bondage to such extrinsic factors as present productivity and future goal-directed behavior. Freed from these bondages of earlier years, the *now* has the possibility of greater creativity.

Unfortunately this radical opportunity for growth, while it stems from increased freedom, is frequently experienced as a threat. Because of our tendency to identify ourselves with our achievements and our past roles, becoming someone new means giving up the known and secure. Writing in *Theology and Pastoral Care*, John Cobb describes the risk involved in creative growth:

> We can let the not-yet transform us only by letting go of what we are. And we must let go of what we are without knowing in advance what we will become. Growth is not the working out of a pattern that we have planned for ourselves. It does not follow lines

that we can predetermine, for it involves the emergence of ways of thinking and feeling that are new. Our plans cannot go beyond the elements that are already present in experience. To allow growth to take place is always a risk. This is why trust is so important. We cannot grow without surrendering the effort to control the future. But to surrender this effort is not to become passive, just to let the powerful forces of the world buffet us about. That would be the opposite of trust in God. That would be to let the world determine everything. That is the way of death. Christian existence is a life of constant decision in the context of the gift of God's presence; it is the continual choosing of life.*

The actions and decisions which effect creativity and directivity are not made utterly without regard for the aims toward which those actions and decisions lead. There has to be at least some glimpse, however faint, of the *what-is-not-yet* in the present moment in order for the novelty of creativity to emerge between the present and the future moment. Without this lure, "things can only repeat the past, and the repetition is never perfect."† This necessity for a glimpse of the *what-could-be*, which serves as a tempting foretaste of the future in the present and makes possible the faithful leap from the present known to the future unknown, presents us with one of the great conceptual dilemmas of old age. Old age may be a time in which there are reduced expectations for either a distant future or present productivity, but the creative possibility of the *now* remains a viable structure. What is missing is some sense of proximate aims, a glimpse of the *what-could-be,* which can lure the creative leap into the future.

Where the growthful possibilities in old age are not seen the result is a state of entropy—a gradual running down of the organism because energizing creativity is lacking. Entropy increases as expectations for novelty and meaningful directivity diminish. You may have heard older people speak of the difficulties of living "with nothing to look forward to." Imagine for a moment what your life might be like if suddenly you found yourself without a single goal you thought worthy of pursuit!

The awareness of specific possibilities for personal development in the near future and the anticipation of their fulfillment provide the goals which encourage creative movement in old age. Church programs could offer just such opportunities in the lives of older members. In the highly mobile society in which many of us live, a foster grandparent program in church or community might provide a valuable resource for younger people while at the same time creating an atmosphere of enjoyable contacts for interested older people. Or consider for a moment the self-esteem which can be strengthened from participation in an oral history program in which memories and experiences from the past are valued and sought out.

The anticipation of something achievable in the immediate future can give an old person a greater opportunity to participate in the process of growth which is integral to directivity. Old age can become, instead of a stagnant pool, a major stage of radical freedom in which expectations and choices encourage new life to emerge.

The Process of Self-Identification

Old age is marked not only by the absence of a distant future and a diminution of the productive present, but also by a unique juncture of circumstances favorable to self-identification. Before we turn to those circumstances in old age which encourage greater self-awareness I would like for you to consider with me a particularly useful definition of *self* developed by Roberto Assagioli, an Italian psychiatrist whose methods are becoming helpful to psychotherapists of many schools.*

The "personal self," Assagioli teaches, is not a physical place in the brain or body. Neither is it a logical construct inferred from the human personality. Rather the personal self results from experiential reality. It involves a reflexive awareness in which the self is aware of itself as the center in which experience takes place— as distinct from the contents of any particular experience. As such it is not to be confused with the conscious personality with which a person often conceptualizes one's self. According to Assagioli:

> The "self," that is to say, the point of pure self-awareness, is often confused with the conscious personality, ... but in reality it is quite different from it. This can be ascertained by the use of careful introspection. The changing *contents* of consciousness (the sensations, thoughts, feelings, etc.) are one thing, while the "I," the self, the *center* of our consciousness is another. From a certain point of view this difference can be compared to that existing between the white lighted area on a screen and the various pictures projected upon it.†

Neither is this experience of the self to be confused with the perceptions of the organism. These perceptions are related to the field of consciousness in which a person is aware of various sensations, images, thoughts, feelings, impulses, and desires. The personal self has the capacity to judge, observe, and analyze all of these elements in the field of consciousness whether they originate from within or without the organism. The personal self is "a point of consciousness and self-awareness, coupled with its realization and the use of its directing will."*

A person may assert, "I am myself," or "I am me," but this realization is often somewhat diffuse because of the individual's identification with certain elements within the field of consciousness; for example, a person may say, "I am depressed," thereby identifying the self with a transitory mood. "Pure self-awareness," however, is not an ordinary experience of everyday life occurring spontaneously of its own accord. It is a center of awareness which can be differentiated from one's performance in the world, so that the sense of "I" or "me" is not so completely identified with the reflected appraisal of others. In the words of Assagiolian psychotherapist Graham Taylor:

> A person is not entirely what he does, or how he behaves, even if his behavior is marked with consistent mistakes and defeats. He is a person facing some defeats, and some mistakes; he is not defeat itself and that only. He can learn to *disidentify* himself from his mistakes and defeats.†

In addition to identifying with elements in the field of consciousness and with the reflected appraisal of others, a person often tends to identify with the roles he or she plays in life, such as "I am a father" or "I am a teacher." But the person is never simply the sum of these various roles because the self is separate, beyond these partial role-identities.‡ After all is separated out, the self remains as a center of consciousness and self-awareness and as a source of strength and growth. The personal self functions as a core of synthesis, a unifying center which is capable of synthesizing behavior and attitudes but is not identified with them.

Assagioli's definition of *self* may not be easy to comprehend, yet the effort is particularly worthwhile for those who work with the aged. The reality of a worthful personal self which is "dis-identified" from any role, mood, success, or failure is an invaluable perspective to the pastor who tries to offer an old person the genuine help needed to adjust effectively to changes in life circumstances.

Actually what I have called the *now* of old age constitutes an especially favorable juncture of circumstances which encourages the process of self-identification and subsequent growth of the spirit. The time-limited nature of most previous role identifications becomes more apparent. Because of retirement a person has much more difficulty identifying with work roles. The parental roles of earlier decades in which enormous amounts of time and energy were invested have, like the work roles, become past history, experienced as presently significant only in the form of memory. These "disidentifications" can help free the older person for a more comprehensive self-identification than was possible in less mature years.

In the earlier decades of life those experiences and roles with which the self most closely identified tended to dominate the self and stifle creative self-awareness. The *now,* however, brings with it a chance for the process of self-identification to accelerate as the parallel process of disidentification takes place. It offers the old person an enormous opportunity for freedom and responsibility. Through creative programs and wise counsel you can be present in your ministry at this crossroads.

Directivity and the creativity it brings need not end at twenty-five, or even forty-five, but can continue into the last decades of life. Take a moment to think about your own life. Consider your ministry. For some of us the issues of aging might serve as a spur for the development of a sense of the *what-is-not-yet,* which grasps possibilities in the creative movement between the present and the future. Others of us might find ourselves encouraged to accelerate the process of self-identification and disidentification as we consider the gifts of radical freedom inherent in old age. Before proceeding to the next chapter you may wish to formulate some hypotheses about how the ideas presented here might be applied in your context of ministry as well as in your personal life.

3. Developmental Crises

"Then old Dr. John and I hiked up another section of mountains until we finally came to a point. The view was magnificent. It was breathtaking. He turned to me and said 'You know if a man lives a full life, he can look twice as far as he can see.' We stood there in silence and I indeed felt that I understood what he meant."
—B. Lewis Barnett, Jr., M.D., *The Extra Dimension of Life*

Erik Erikson and other theoreticians in life-span developmental psychology have seen maturation coming about as the result of various crises in the life cycle. At the point of crisis the person has an opportunity either to move in the direction of health and wholeness or to stabilize at an immature level of development which continues to impede growth for the remainder of life. Within this frame of reference a developmental crisis is not an event to be avoided—it carries with it an opportunity for growth and personal enhancement. In the earlier years of life these times of relative crisis—which have been termed stages of emotional development—seem to occur with relative predictability and are closely related to physical development as well as age.

Developmental Complexities in Middle Age

As a person advances in age, environmental factors play an increasingly important role in determining which stage of development is experienced. This means that in adulthood—which stretches from the twenties to the century mark and beyond—age and physical development (or deterioration) gradually play a less important role when compared to the other contributing factors, such as family and job.

Furthermore development itself becomes more complex in the middle years as it is now more closely aligned with emotional and spiritual experience. As a result it becomes virtually impossible to predict which stage (if stages in fact even exist) a person is moving through during, for example, the decade of the fifties.

Sally H. is a fifty-two-year-old grandmother of four, whose own adult children live within a thirty-minute drive from her home. When the last child left home for college, Sally herself enrolled in college in order to finish a degree interrupted many years previously. She was fascinated by how her interests had changed over the years. When first at the university, years before, she had planned to major in home economics. Now she had finished a competitive program in business, majoring in real estate, and was managing her own small firm, which specialized in the sales of smaller homes. Combined with her husband's income, they now have more money than either ever dreamed possible. All in all, Sally finds her life a real challenge.

Thomas T. is a fifty-two-year-old father of two girls, both of whom are in junior high school. Because of his seniority, thirty years at the same factory, and a generous pension plan sponsored by his union, Tom is planning to retire in the next four months. He and his wife have both looked forward to this day since they made a down payment on a little place out in the country several years ago. Before they can move from the city, however, Tom has a lot of work to do on the older home, which needs rewiring and a new roof. He plans to build a workshop with fluorescent lights and a heater for the long winter months. The girls hate to leave their friends in the city but at the same time are looking forward to getting their own horse. The only "fly in the ointment" is the pain Tom has recently begun to experience in his chest when he exerts himself strenuously. He hasn't been to the doctor yet, and hopes that it will disappear of its own accord.

These two cases remind us that people of the same age may be grappling with wholly different developmental issues and that a particular issue that becomes relevant for one person at age forty may not be equally relevant for another person until the age of sixty. This complexity of emotional development in the last half of life enhances the challenge of a creative ministry seeking to meet people at their several points of need.

Coping with Physical Aging

Crises of emotional development encountered in the mid-years might be thought of as "silent crises" because they are relatively undramatic and any ensuing damage may not become apparent until later. These crises, however, particularly if growth attends them, can be significant for old age.

For many of us the initial encoutner with our own aging comes at the point of physique. The encounter with our own body is often difficult, even painful:

> This witty, not very profound, slender woman with hardly any lines, no pouches or sags, her hair skillfully cut and discreetly highlighted, who moved lithely and made love voluptuously, could not, surely, be a grandmother? Shawls, caps, knitting? Granny? Grandma? It was ridiculous.
>
> But true . . . .
>
> She studied her hand and her arm where the sleeve fell away from it. There was flab under the upper arm, and on her forearm the muscles seemed to show more than they used to as though the flesh were receding. Her hands were still beautiful, but the skin had become a little too fine. And were those freckles or—she blanched but faced the terrible term—age spots?*

Youthful persons depend heavily on physically-based powers for success. From the star quarterback who plays heroically despite a fever, and the student who studies all night before an exam, to the young mother who depends on sheer stamina to care for her three sick preschoolers, the role of physical endurance is apparent.

Somewhere in the mid-range of life, however, persons reach a critical juncture where the realities of their own aging challenge them to adopt new ways of mastering the problems of living. Not everyone responds easily to such a challenge. Robert C. Peck points to the often uphill struggle between the old, physique-based values and the new ways of coping with life:

> Some people cling to physical powers, both as their chief "tool" for coping with life, and as the most important element in their value-hierarchy, especially in their self-definition. Since physical powers inevitably decline, such people tend to grow increasingly depressed, bitter, or otherwise unhappy as they grow older. Moreover, they may become increasingly ineffective in their work roles and social roles, if they try to rely on physical powers which they no longer possess.†

Successful aging involves the substitution of wisdom for physique as the dominant means of accomplishing life's many tasks. The successful middle-ager discovers in the accumulation of life experience a valuable asset which can be judiciously used to help accomplish more than would ever be possible by sheer exertion alone. To value our wisdom-based powers above our physique-based powers means to appreciate our head more than our muscle. We then evaluate tasks at hand in light of the available options and finite resources rather than simply plunging ahead in frenetic and often inefficient activity.

Dealing with Change

Movement through the life cycle involves continuous change. People are born, grow up, get married, and have children. Children start kindergarten, change schools, graduate, find full-time jobs, and get out on their own. Recreational interests develop, flourish, then gradually decline. Friends move away or die. Then too there are the job changes, relocations, promotions, retirement. Each transformation brings different responsibilities and new concerns. Change is so much with us that we sometimes forget it is there.

Each change in life circumstances can be experienced as an opportunity for growth or an occasion for loss. Indeed each change is likely to involve both. One of the most important developmental issues for middle age is to balance our inner accounting books in favor of growth.

It is in the middle years that our patterns of dealing with change become habitual. Through the youthful decades a pattern of slow loss in one's inner account book may be subtly disguised and thereby go unnoticed. In middle age, however, as the pace of change accelerates, an accumulating deficit unfavorable to growth may begin to emerge. This can become acute in the later years. How we deal with the mental and emotional challenges of change during the mid-years is thus of paramount importance for old age, when the ability to handle change becomes crucial for successful functioning, indeed for survival.

The capacity to endow current activities, interests, and persons with value and significance is referred to in psychological terms as cathexis. A highly cathected idea (or person, activity, or relationship) is one in which the thinker has invested a lot of meaning and energy—and consequently prizes more highly than an idea of low cathexis about which the thinker is more dispassionate. Cathexis significantly affects the way in which we adapt to the inexorable changes of life. Cathetic flexibility, the capacity to shift significant emotional investments from one activity or person to another, becomes increasingly important with advancing age. If in middle age there is such emotional rigidity that a person finds it extremely difficult to value new relationships and activities, then old age is likely to be experienced as an emotional wasteland: old friends die and are never replaced, and new activities do not take the place of those given up because of new circumstances.

Roger T. grew up in a small midwestern community. Following high school and a stint in the army he went to work at the town's one large factory and married Pam, a local girl. Through effort and determination Roger advanced within the plant until, in his forties, he became the purchasing agent. The parent company offered him a significant promotion to that of assistant purchasing agent in the home firm on the West Coast. After some agonizing, he accepted the new position. Pam had become enthusiastic about the expanded job possibilities for her, and since their children were out of the nest they felt fairly free to make the move.

At first Roger was so enthusiastic about his new responsibilities that he scarcely noticed what he was missing, but gradually the deficits built up. He and Pam visited several churches but always left somewhat disappointed because, as he put it, "they seem so different from our church back home." Roger had been an avid fisherman, but no one seemed very interested in fresh-water fishing, and he found the ocean terrifying.

Roger and Pam took their vacations "back home" to see the kids and visit with old friends. Everyone seemed happy enough to see him, but something was different now—as if he lived in a different world. He even found himself wondering if he wanted to wait until retirement before moving back.

While Roger is still valiantly trying to adapt to his new environment he is having a hard time with cathetic flexibility. Roger's accounts are not yet complete, but he is finding it difficult to endow his new circle of friends and activities with the same degree of significance as those back home — "things are so different out here."

Rigidity and Flexibility

As we accumulate life experiences, our attitude toward our own personal history becomes an important factor in continued personal growth. That attitude can be marked by either mental rigidity or mental flexibility.

Our own unique life-course of choice, successes, and mistakes provides each of us with a set of solutions which either seemed to work in the past or are thought likely to have worked had they been applied. We may regard these as fixed solutions always ready at hand, to be applied whenever the current situation seems reminiscent of the past. Instead of seeing each present issue in terms of a new set of circumstances never before encountered in precisely the same way, and therefore calling for an equally thoughtful and uncommon response, we respond to virtually all of life's current problems on the basis of answers which were appropriate for situations which no longer exist.

Unfortunately, the stereotype of old age as a time of such mental rigidity misses the mark by several decades. While the habit of deriving fixed guidelines for life from past experience may be most noticeable only in the later years, it was surely being formed back in the mid-years. Its consequences in later years can be tragic: current problems have to be avoided since the mentally rigid person is no longer capable of creative problem-solving and tends to withdraw from all but the most routine aspects of life.

By way of contrast, persons who are mentally flexible make full use of past experiences but are not bound to those answers which have already worked. They do not automatically consign bygone solutions to the dustbin of history without examination, but regard the past simply as one source of potentially useful ideas for possible solutions, to be explored along with other ideas from the sphere of creative imagination and the store of solutions in contemporary use. An attitude of mental flexibility means continued transformation and growth as new mysteries are encountered and tentative solutions tried out.

Anne S. had worked for many years in the library of a small college widely noted for its academic excellence and superb library holdings. She had been involved in most areas of librarianship over the years, learning quickly despite her lack of graduate professional training. Now at age fifty-six she made an important decision—to pursue that graduate degree. Because of her excellent record and academic promise she was granted a sabbatical to enroll in a major university with an excellent program in library science.

No one was surprised at Anne's decision to go back to school. Colleagues knew her as an innovative, creative, professionally-minded person who was always looking for better and more efficient procedures to improve the quality of service. In graduate school her papers had an added measure of depth, as she balanced off her new learning with her years of experience. Her peers in school, however, scarcely even noticed her gray hair as they were challenged by her innovative analysis of problems presented in class.

Before graduation Anne received an offer from an internationally renowned library noted for its professional challenge and prestige. To go back to her old college meant that she could apply her new knowledge in a familiar setting at a considerable raise in pay, but now that looked sort of dull to her. Her classmates in library science were not surprised when she took the new position. Anne was that sort of person—creative, solid, and open to the future.

Who knows what old age may hold for Anne? About all we know for sure is that now, in the last decade of middle age, she seems securely established in her attitude of mental flexibility. Already at fifty-six she is in the habit of using her past experiences not as a set of inflexible rules to be applied rigidly to current problems, but more as a set of provisional solutions which might have some application in new situations. If Anne's present trajectory continues into old age—and I bet it does—she will continue to be known for those same qualities which make her stand out now.

Mental flexibility, like mental rigidity, is a habit of problem-solving which emerges in middle age and has a decisive impact on experience in old age. The mentally flexible person does not need to avoid unusual experiences which call for novel solutions. The unknown is not a threat because one does not have to operate on the basis of a finite number of solutions from the past, solutions which may in fact be irrelevant. Mental flexibility encourages a spirit of openness and growth in old age, while mental rigidity seems to be associated with intellectual stagnation and eventual withdrawal.

Crises of Old Age

Although the developmental processes and complexities of the mid-years have continuing impact, old age itself is not a period of stale inactivity in which we merely reap what was sown in our encounters with the mid-years crises. The issues remaining toward the end of life are some of the most significant of the entire human life cycle, and the manner in which these final crises are handled will have an impact on personhood and even physical survival. All that has gone before has been a kind of training ground for the final showdown between the internal mechanisms leading to meaning and growth and those which lead to anomie and entropy. Only those persons who have been fortunate enough to come through their previous developmental crises unscathed and intact arrive at old age equipped for these last encounters.

As in the earlier stages of life, those individuals with the basic integrity of their personality uncompromised by savage disease or the cruel vicissitudes of life have the greatest opportunities for growth and creativity. This does not mean that a person impaired by disease or other negative circumstances cannot be creative or participate in continued growth. On the contrary, given the level of their functional capacities such persons may be as creative as anyone else. As long as a single shred of personal integrity remains, aged persons continue to make an impression, however slight, on their life-course and on other persons whose lives intersect with theirs.

While our understanding of the developmental crises of old age applies mainly to persons of relatively good health and sound mind, it is still relevant for a broad spectrum of persons within a wide range of life circumstances. Although no one can gauge in advance the psychological impact of such experiences, the person who has faced the fact of physical aging fairly early and has developed some measure of cathetic and mental flexibility would seem well equipped to meet successfully whatever crises old age has to offer: the loss of cherished roles, the onset of physical disabilities, even approaching death.

Role Changes

In the previous chapter we spoke of self-identification in the last decades of life. During this period many of the roles which were previously assumed have begun to fall away—less significance is attached to them and opportunities are fewer for enacting them in day-to-day activities. While this process of disidentification is often experienced as a sense of loss, it can also bring with it a consequent increase in opportunity for a more pure self-identification, in which the self is no longer confused with the transient roles of life. The self can come to be experienced as the decisional power which synthesizes and coordinates roles and is not identical with or exhausted by any of them.

For many people in our society work has been the significant preoccupation throughout the middle years, and almost inadvertently the self has been closely identified with a particular work role. Where this identification has been especially close, the anticipation of retirement is experienced as a threat, and actual withdrawal from work, when it comes, brings a sense of loss. For the person who has worked to establish role diversity, however, retirement is not so likely to be traumatic.

Role diversity is not so much the substitution of another role or roles for the work role as an active process on the part of the self whereby the self synthesizes new roles out of previously fragmentary and undeveloped roles. Often these new roles are more free to emerge following retirement. Personal worth is then experienced in a wider variety of settings which utilize a greater repertoire of behaviors than was previously possible with a predominantly work-role preoccupation. As a consequence of this role diversity, satisfaction and worth come to be more closely related to the process of synthesis itself, instead of depending on one particular role or combination of roles.

Robert G. had been a successful attorney for forty years when he first retired from his law firm. He had talked about retirement and all of the wonderful things he was going to do when that day came, but had never made any realistic plans. The first few weeks of his retirement were spent in assembling an elaborate set of woodworking tools for the many projects he had been saving up. Then it was off for a month's vacation with his wife. After several months of relatively hard work in the wood shop by day and, for him, rather heavy drinking at night, Robert finally admitted that he was more miserable than he had ever been in his life. He began to think about returning to the firm, even in a reduced capacity. To make a long story short, Robert returned to his firm for several more years of active and productive work before retiring again, only to return once more to the practice of law. He died without ever having successfully retired—still a man driven by his inner needs to produce, and preoccupied with his role as an attorney.

Persons who are not self-employed professional or business people may not have the same easy exit or reentry to the job market as did Robert. For them retirement usually sticks, and an adjustment must be made to this fact. If role diversity already exists, then the transition to the nonworking years can be an enjoyable and growthful experience instead of a threat to be avoided.

Some years ago I had the good fortune to become acquainted with a man who has continued to represent for me the epitome of successful retirement. My friend Reggie retired from teaching at the age of sixty-two. He had been regarded throughout his career as an extremely creative and energetic classroom educator. I got to know him several years after his retirement, but I am sure that retirement itself presented no insurmountable problems for him.

When I met Reggie he had several interesting hobbies, each of which was a challenge to him. They ranged over a number of diverse fields of interest.

In earlier years he had played and coached in the community baseball league. Now, instead of merely coaching one team, he had become a "coach's coach" who would help with morale problems or troubleshoot a better way to teach a particularly difficult technique. He enjoyed himself immensely in this role and found that his own experience as a former player and coach was a valuable asset.

Reggie had always secretly wanted to be an auto mechanic, although he hardly knew the difference between a screwdriver and a pair of pliers. He worked out an arrangement with a local garage in which he would lend them a hand if they would explain what they were doing and why, so he could learn the rudiments of auto mechanics. It was a real victory for him when he correctly diagnosed his car's engine problem and successfully performed the needed tune-up.

Reggie had always bowled in a local league and still did, with real enjoyment. He enjoyed the fun of the game as much as he had once enjoyed the competition, so being in a slower league didn't bother him a bit.

Word collecting had been a hobby for years. Whenever Reggie encountered a new word he copied down the source and the context, and then looked it up in the library's Oxford dictionary. Since he read widely, he had quite an impressive collection.

Arthritis has recently begun to slow Reggie considerably, but his flexibility and diversity have enabled him to adjust well. Today instead of bowling he is tutoring high school students, and he still works at his word collection.

Reggie is clearly well advanced in the process we have referred to as self-identification. I picture him as a relaxed student. In every situation there is something for him to discover or learn about some activity, about life, or about himself. Though most of us have to work hard to achieve role diversity, for Reggie it seems to happen quite naturally.

Physical Disability

Unfortunately, for many people old age is associated with some form of physical impairment, be it a crippling arthritis or "just" a hearing loss. Although age itself is rarely a causal factor, it is safe to assume that the longer we live, the greater becomes the likelihood that we will experience some measure of disability.

Much can be done in the way of rehabilitation and physical therapy to help the healing process along, if society provides the means and the elderly make full use of them. Old people should not stoically accept physical impairment, nor should they employ psychological denial as a means of coping with disability. Yet certain losses are clearly irreversible and can have a most significant impact on the personality, challenging self-definition at its core.

For whatever reasons, old age does seem to bring a reduction in recuperative powers. A four-year-old boy may run a fever of 104°, and a few hours later be recovered and hard at play. His grandmother, on the other hand, may take a week or longer to gain her strength back after a similar infection. This does not mean that the elderly person is more sickly or fragile, only that what is normal recovery time for a four-year-old is abnormal for a senior citizen.

The difficulty of adjusting to a longer recovery time, however, is slight compared to that of contending with the accumulated aches and pains of bursitis and arthritis or other chronic illnesses which impinge on our lifestyle and restrict our normal range of activity. Such illnesses add up to a challenge to self-definition that is without parallel in the younger decades of life. If our sense of well-being has rested primarily on physical health, then old age with its cumulative physical insults is likely to be experienced as a time of downward physical spiral in which the human spirit is almost crushed.

For those whose sense of well-being is based upon physical health, old age becomes a period of overriding preoccupation with the body, in which the slightest variation in bodily functions is a cause for alarm or undue concern. If I, as an old person, identify my "self" totally with my body, then my aching joints mean that "I" am not doing too well. My morale suffers and I lose the capacity to invest life-energy in the world outside my body. The following excerpt from an Ann Landers column presents a younger person's view of such preoccupation with the body:

> Dear Ann Landers:
> I have never written to you before, but after I read the letter signed "Lonesome" I knew my time had come.
> My in-laws are also "lonesome" — at least that's what they tell everybody. We hear from many people that they complain constantly about how we ignore them and how hurt they are. It burns me up.
> Last Sunday my husband and I and the kids went to see them and it was the same old story. Grandma and Grandpa talked about nothing but how sick they are, how much they suffer (she with backaches and he with rheumatism in his legs). It is a real contest to see who is in worse shape.
> Then they tell us for the fiftieth time about how bad their operations were — hers two years ago for a tumor, his five years ago for a hernia.
> They are so self-centered it is awful. Never a question about the children or my husband's job or my interests. All they want to do is talk about themselves and their sicknesses.
> Also, whenever we go to see them they greet us with, "We didn't think you were coming."
> I wonder how many other "lonesome" parents there are around? If so maybe there's a good reason their children don't visit them more often.
> —Cause and Effect
>
> Dear Cause:
> There are plenty around, and I've heard from dozens of them. Your signature was most appropriate. Whenever you get an "effect" like the one described in your letter there's got to be a "cause." Thanks for writing.*

While the letter is almost a caricature, it does point up what preoccupation with the body can be like for some people in old age. Fortunately we all know that the life cycle does not end this way for a majority of persons. Pain and discomfort cannot be eliminated, but most people choose to relate to their aches in a different way, through what might be called body transcendence.

Persons who have chosen to transcend their bodily aches and pains experience no less discomfort in old age than others, who worry unduly about their bodies, but their sense of well-being seems to rest on something other than physical comfort alone. If I, for example, base my sense of happiness on rewarding human relationships and creative mental activities, then physical discomfort is not experienced as a threat to "me," but more as a problem to be solved or an impediment to be skirted in the movement toward proximate goals.

Grandma, as she was affectionately known by people at the nursing home, was approaching 100 years of age. She wore thick eye glasses and could see well enough to read the *New York Times,* which she did daily as she sipped her morning coffee, an activity which took both hands since both were so grossly deformed. Because of her arthritis, turning the pages took a great deal of effort, but Grandma had discovered a way which worked for her over the years, and besides, "What's a little extra time anyway?" she would say with a twinkle in her eyes.

There were days when Grandma didn't want to get out of bed because of a flare-up of her arthritis, with knees and hands painfully swollen. But the next day she might be sitting in her rocking chair knitting a scarf for a great-great-grandchild who lived hundreds of miles away. Her hands were so deformed that someone else had to place the knitting needles properly between her fingers. She usually seemed to be working on a garment to present to a little one whose next visit to the nursing home was some months away. While I never met any of Grandma's family, I suspect that receiving a knitted garment from her was an important event, a token of her love treasured far beyond its utilitarian value.

Grandma had every reason imaginable to be preoccupied with her body, but in the many hours we spent together I never detected such an attitude. It was not that she denied the reality of her condition—she just seemed more interested in her family, the newspaper, and her current project.

For persons such as Grandma, who have faced many of life's challenges and possess a deeply-rooted sense of body transcendance, there are few things in life that can disrupt the healthy sense of selfhood. Death may have such a power, as may the threat of mental deterioration in which the uniqueness of one's personality is lost beneath an avalanche of grave insults. Yet even these two potential crises are likely to be encountered successfully by persons who have experienced emotional growth throughout the entire life cycle.

Death

The certainty of approaching death occasions the last significant developmental crisis in the human life cycle. How this final necessity is anticipated and dealt with remains the last creative opportunity for each of us—and probably the most difficult. We may say, glibly perhaps, that death at the conclusion of a long, vibrant, and growthful life has a different meaning than death at, say, nineteen years of age. Yet death always packs a powerful sting, regardless of the age at which it comes, and regardless of any preparations that may have been made. Consider the experience of Simone de Beauvoir at the death of her mother:

> I did not understand that one might sincerely weep for a relative, a grandfather aged seventy and more. If I met a woman of fifty overcome with sadness because she had just lost her mother, I thought her neurotic: we are all mortal; at eighty you are quite old enough to be one of the dead . . .
>
> But it is not true. You do not die from being born, nor from having lived, nor from old age. You die from something. The knowledge that because of her age my mother's life must soon come to an end did not lessen the horrible surprise: she had sarcoma. Cancer, thrombosis, pneumonia: it is as violent and unforeseen as an engine stopping in the middle of the sky. My mother encouraged one to be optimistic when, crippled with arthritis and dying, she asserted the infinite value of each instant; but her vain tenaciousness also ripped and tore the reassuring curtain of everyday triviality. There is no such thing as a natural death: nothing that happens to a man is ever natural, since his presence calls the world into question. All men must die: but for every man his death is an accident and, even if he knows it and consents to it, an unjustifiable violation.*

While the actual moment of death may come as a "horrible surprise" for those "of an age to die," the fact that it will come sooner rather than later is difficult to deny. Death is not an unexpected event. In the presence of degrading and painful infirmities it may even be welcome. Sometimes plans are made in anticipation of its coming, plans affecting the prolongation of life in the event of lingering illness, or for the distribution of personal property, or for last rites. For the person who has lived with emotional integrity, death itself does not have the power to terrify. It is anticipated and participated in to the fullest extent possible in keeping with one's previous values and orientation to life.

Many aged persons have puzzled over the meaning of their life and already reached some resolution concerning the termination of conscious personality as we know it. For persons of a religious orientation this resolution might be expressed in biblical terms, such as the hope of resurrection. Others might express it in more general theological/philosophical terms if these are more harmonious with the person's life experience and outlook. Regardless of the terminology or the orientation, the struggle to comprehend and incorporate death meaningfully into the life cycle continues until the task is accomplished.

Young people thinking about personal death often assume that the dying person is preoccupied with immortalizing the conscious personality. Such self-absorption occurs with less frequency than might be expected. The aged person who is thus self-preoccupied experiences the world as an unsafe place in which to lose one's grip on life. The only knowable immortality remaining after death lies in the finite creations of the productive phases of the life cycle. These productions afford the only avenue for controlling how one will be evaluated after death. Thus one's own *place* in history becomes more important than one's having perpetuated the historical process as such through participation in a culture. The composer who is self-absorbed, for example, regards the immortalization of a personal composition as more important than having carried forward a musical tradition which will continue to bring pleasure in unknown ways to generations yet unborn.

But one person is so small in the face of the inexorable process of time. Self-absorption makes death the enemy which cuts short the remaining time. Life can only end in despair over the time not available or used and the roads not chosen or travelled. To shoulder the burdens which go with self-absorption in old age is an impossible task.

Where aged persons are aware of having built their life on a larger foundation, self-transcendence can supplant self-absorption. If one's basic bedrock values have been proven true in the test of life and death, then one has participated in the perpetuation of a value system which is larger than any individual life can actualize and which will endure, one believes, to the end of time. Then self can safely release its grip on life, knowing that through

4. Reminiscence

It is said that once upon a time the people of a remote mountain village used to sacrifice and eat their old men. A day came when there was not a single old man left, and the traditions were lost. They wanted to build a great house for the meetings of the assembly, but when they came to look at the tree-trunks that had been cut for that purpose no one could tell the top from the bottom: if the timber were placed the wrong way up, it would set off a series of disasters. A young man said that if they promised never to eat the old men any more, he would be able to find a solution. They promised. He brought his grandfather, whom he had hidden; and the old man taught the community to tell top from bottom.
—Simone de Beauvoir, *The Coming of Age*

In chapter 2 we spoke of early old age as a time for "catching up," a time when individuals seem unusually sensitive to their own past. Persons in the fifties and sixties find themselves spontaneously reaching back over the decades to make contact with memories which are reexperienced with surprising vitality in the here and now. Frequently these experiences of reminiscence are so dynamic and meaningful that the individual wants to share them with another person.

Pastors routinely observe and even participate in many such experiences involving reminiscence. You can probably recall more than a few such occasions just within the past month. One might have been with your youth group, which while planning a camping trip found their greatest delight in talking about last year's expedition. Or you might recall a committee meeting in which someone "got sidetracked" and started talking about the whys and hows of a tradition going back many years in your church. Or you might have found yourself restlessly stealing a glance at your watch while a parishioner was engrossed in telling you a story of something significant that happened many years ago.

45

After you have recalled a few such encounters with reminiscence try to remember how you *felt* on those occasions. Were you bored? angered? interested? involved? perhaps even challenged?

In similar situations I have sometimes noticed that my own feelings were those of frustration. I was frustrated that the youth group was not more businesslike in making decisions about this year's trip; frustrated at the seemingly interminable "war stories" which slowed a committee's deliberations; even frustrated that I had to listen to another long tale which I didn't fully understand, couldn't appreciate, and didn't know how to respond to meaningfully. Reminiscence on such occasions seemed more like an intrusion or a mere pastime than a matter of meaningful communication—though even then I wondered about its fascination and function when the reminiscence was mine rather than "theirs."

My need to be seen as a loving pastor who cared about people usually meant that I patiently tried to move the meeting along without being too offensive and hurting someone's feelings, or I listened patiently to the individual's story and made some socially acceptable reply without getting significantly involved with the person. Often I marvelled at the "inefficiency" of committees or wondered why someone was talking *to me* about something which happened so long ago. Perhaps your reaction on such occasions has been quite different from mine, your feelings less negative. In any case you can probably identify at least partially with my feelings of frustration and share my surprise in the growthful discovery that such experiences are indeed worth pursuing.

Some of my frustration obviously stemmed from the fact that I simply had never thought of reminiscence as a meaningful activity, one to be understood, appreciated, and fostered. But somewhere along the way I found myself coming to think of reminiscence in just those terms, as a supremely worthwhile activity, fully as deserving of pastoral attention as any of the group activities and committee processes in which it sometimes occurred. No longer did reminiscence seem like a waste of time. It actually opened up valuable new ways of achieving intimacy with persons, ways which had seldom been possible for me in my ministerial busyness. It encouraged individual emotional growth by helping persons to "catch up" and integrate past experiences into present functioning. Surprisingly, it even enhanced group cohesiveness and functioning.

A Meaningful Lifetime Activity

Reminiscence is the natural process of mental recollection experienced by all people in all cultures and all walks of life. It is a spontaneous activity occurring without anticipation or rehearsal. It may be pursued in solitude or shared by persons who have had similar experiences. Usually it involves not vague perceptions or sensations but concrete memories associated with specific past events.

Often the emotions attendant upon the original experiences surface anew during the recollections. Awareness then may focus on those emotions and thoughts which arise in the process itself. "My, my, I didn't know it affected me *that* much"—such a common expression indicates that the reminiscer, so far from dealing with the past event alone, is attempting to make sense out of the original experience in the light of current circumstances.

Sometimes the impact of the reminiscence is expressed in terms of the time that has elapsed since the event: "It seems like it happened only yesterday. . . . Has it really been forty years?" Such comments probably indicate the immediacy and power of the particular memory as much as the surprise over the actual passage of time. Sometimes a person may acknowledge the significance of the past event by pondering out loud: "I wonder what my life would have been like if that hadn't happened."

The need to root any particular reminiscence meaningfully in the life cycle probably varies with the impact of the perceived event on the person's life. The greater its significance the more one tries to relate it to a time line or a historical sequence of events leading up to and including the present.

Thus reminiscence includes two major components: the basic memory itself with its affective and cognitive charges of energy, and the evaluative process which tries to make sense of the original event. Both factors are important in the total act of reminiscence. Together they give it its meaning.

Such meaningful activity is not restricted to the elderly. Reminiscing takes place across much of the life-span. An adolescent on the way home from school observes workers from the electric company trimming a favorite oak and is poignantly reminded of times spent years before with the neighborhood gang building a treehouse in that old oak. A mother learns of her daughter's disappointment over a broken date and promptly reexperiences feelings of hurt and anger from her own youthful past. Recently as we were following a pickup truck down the highway, even our four-year-old son engaged in a form of reminiscence: "Daddy, Uncle Lee and I took his truck for a ride. You know, the red one? I sat in the back with the bicycle [said with obvious glee]. We went for a ride on it near the big trees. It was fun! When will I see Uncle Lee again?" The remembered event had taken place when David was only two.

Most persons entering early old age have probably reminisced throughout much of their life. Although the process for them is not new, the quality of the experience is inclined to be different now that they have entered another unique phase in the life cycle.

Social expectation and approval probably helps loosen the elderly person's internalized barriers to the experience and expression of reminiscence. The need for social sham and pretense is also reduced—old people find it easier to be honest with themselves and others. Then there is the concurrent process of disidentification taking place whereby the self becomes increasingly differentiated from previously significant roles. Perhaps, too, the distinctive sense of time—the long past and uncertain future—contributes to the creation of a qualitative difference. Whatever the reasons, reminiscence can surely be a significant element in the total experience of early old age. In fact some research indicates that persons who reminisce freely may even live longer than those who do not.

Clearly reminiscence is a natural activity found in most persons who are healthy and well adjusted. It should not be associated with mental rigidity or "living in the past." So far from being discredited or suppressed, it should be actively encouraged among all age levels, particularly among those who are moving through early old age.

Perspectives on Reminiscence

The process of reminiscing actually includes a variety of activities. These can be grouped into meaningful categories that may illuminate their similarities and differences. We will focus particularly on three perspectives, each of which gives us a slightly different view of the process, thereby enhancing our ability to facilitate those activities likely to prove beneficial in any given case. We may think of these three perspectives in terms of qualities on a polar continuum which overlap, mingle, merge, and later become distinct again, much as the colors of a rainbow merge and then differentiate themselves before merging again.

Recreational/Therapeutic

It may be helpful to think of reminiscence as primarily recreational or primarily therapeutic in nature. Either one results in a greater measure of wholeness for the reminiscer.

In modern times recreation has come to mean a refreshing and renewing play activity which punctuates the usual routines of life. Play is more than an escape; it is a restorative process which enables the person to experience anew the possibilities of creativity in healthy diversions. Therapy, by contrast, seems to communicate more of a remedial process which enables the participant to resume life without the previously experienced blocks or deficits.

Recreational reminiscence would tend to be light and fun, while therapeutic reminiscence would tend toward work and effort, even pain. Therapeutic reminiscence would be closer to a counseling activity, while recreational reminiscence would approach the quality of an enjoyable, yet engrossing game. Both are most likely to take place in an interpersonal context, with other people as listeners and participants.

Shared/Solitary

One may think of reminiscence as occurring somewhere on a continuum which runs from an interpersonal, shared activity at one extreme to an introspective, nonverbal process in the person's own consciousness at the other extreme. The former might be a group activity, while the latter might take place in strict isolation from other people.

A middle position would be that of the reminiscence which is generated within one person but then discussed with another. In this middle area the listener may participate empathically without ever having had an experience similar to that of the reminiscer. Indeed for this very reason the roles of listener and reminiscer can sometimes be exchanged—to the benefit of both.

Enhancing Distance/Enhancing Intimacy

It is possible to think of reminiscence as serving either to increase interpersonal intimacy or to enhance the distance between persons. Where intimacy increases, there are likely to be more of the qualities present which are found in a shared activity. Where interpersonal distance increases, there are likely to be more of the qualities which are isolating and introversive. Storytelling can mean distancing—if it is largely a pastime in which affect is absent and the listener only minimally involved at the point of providing a cue for beginning or ending the activity.

Functions of Reminiscence

Within any one period of reminiscence a variety of valuable psychological functions are being fulfilled to a greater or lesser degree. Three of the more important ones are time parity, dissonance reduction, and life review. Time parity facilitates interpersonal communication. Dissonance reduction and life review, while they can take place in an interpersonal context, refer for the most part to what happens within the reminiscer.

Time Parity

Johnny Wilkinson is a ten-year-old Cub Scout whose den has been visiting the residents in a nearby nursing home once a month. Last month the boys put on an original skit and invited everyone to attend. At first the players had seemed a little timid when they looked out on the packed auditorium, but they soon got into their act and really hammed it up in response to audience laughter. Afterwards the Cubs were surprised that the residents had prepared lemonade and cookies for them. At the reception

Johnny seemed to hit it off pretty well with Mr. Quiggle, an eighty-four-year-old resident in a wheel chair.

This month, after the wiener roast, Johnny visited again with Mr. Quiggle, figuring they wouldn't be back until fall when school reopened. From Johnny's perspective their visit went something like this:

Mr. Q. Johnny, you were really funny in your costume last month. Did you make it yourself?

J. Almost. My brother and father helped shape the nose. All of the den helped paint the mask.

Mr. Q. They said that you won't be back for a while. School must be ending.

J. Yeah. Next week we are through. I can hardly wait.

Mr. Q. What are you going to do?

J. Just mess around. Maybe visit my cousins or something.

Mr. Q. Where do they live?

J. Anniston [about 100 miles away].

Mr. Q. I hope you have a good time. When I was about your age I got to visit relatives up on Sand Mountain. My brother and I rode the train up there and everything. You ever ridden on a train?

J. No.

Mr. Q. It was exciting. We almost got off at the wrong stop. It took almost the entire morning.

J. To get to Sand Mountain?

Mr. Q. It seemed a lot longer. We had to stop at every little crossroad and let someone off or pick up another passenger.

J. We can get to Anniston in an hour and a half.

Mr. Q. What are you going to do when you get there?

J. I dunno. Mess around. Go swimming. Maybe we can camp out or something. It's fun.

Mr. Q. I bet. I remember we used to go skinny-dipping when I was your age. We had this clay bank that led down to the swimming hole and we'd make a slide and get it all wet and slippery. Then we'd slide down into the water with a splash: "plonk." We must've left a pound of

> hide on that bank. There was always a rock or a root or something sticking up. I'd try to go fast and still miss the root. It was great.
>
> J.   I think they've got a slide at the swimming pool now. It should open in another week.
>
> Mr. Q. Send me a picture of you on the slide. That sounds like more fun than a clay bank [laughing]. . . .

One function of reminiscence emerges here quite clearly. Although almost seventy-four years separate Johnny and Mr. Quiggle in age, and the old man is no longer physically active, they develop a sense of rapport over common activities they shared when both were about ten years of age. Mr. Quiggle establishes a time parity, or equality, by telling a story from his past which places him at about the same age as Johnny and shows him involved in about the same sorts of activities that Johnny will engage in this summer. Had Johnny been seventeen years of age, Mr. Quiggle might well have found himself reminiscing instead about football or a part-time job.

Expressions such as "When I was your age . . ." are the older person's attempts to create a sense of time equality.* The older person is saying in effect: "I can relate to being ten years old (or thirty-five). Don't let the years separate us. Let's talk as if we were equals sharing common experiences. I'm neither superior or irrelevant, just interested."

Dissonance Reduction

In adulthood each of us attempts to establish and maintain a certain consistency between our view of our own self (our self-concept) and the evaluations we—or others—make of our behavior. When we become aware of a major incongruity between the person we believe ourselves to be and some aspect of a particular behavior, then cognitive dissonance is said to exist. For example, dissonance comes into being when the self-concept "I am a loving person" confronts behavior which is evaluated as "a mean, spiteful action." Being in a state of cognitive dissonance is such an uncomfortable experience that we strive almost automatically to disown the dissonant element, thereby establishing a new consistency between self-concept and behavior.

Persons who reach early old age in a state of relative wholeness are likely to have built up a considerable resource of memories which tell them that they are indeed worthy, loved, and interesting persons. Over the years other people in work, family, religious, and recreational contexts have responded positively to the now elderly persons in a variety of circumstances. Healthy older persons are also likely to perceive that valued aspects of their personalities and lifestyles have remained fairly consistent through time: "Who I am today is consistent with who I was last year." Until now society has tended to reinforce such positive self-concepts with paychecks and the prestige accorded significant roles.

In early old age, however, dissonance often crops up. The elderly person may think: "At one time I was active, loved, and hard-working . . . at present I am old, retired, and alone." When coupled with a persistent desire to live up to the original self-concept, the present perception leads to dissonance.*

The uncomfortable state of dissonance can be alleviated in several ways. We may, for example, revise our self-concept by recognizing that we are not *really* who we thought ourselves to be. Some of those seemingly alien qualities in our behavior— which caused the dissonance in the first place—may be incorporated into our self-concept; thus when the self-concept "I am a logically consistent person" is confronted with a piece of absurd or irrational behavior, the self-concept can appropriately be amended: "I *strive* to be a logically consistent person."

Unfortunately in old age many behavioral elements which give rise to dissonance are not of one's own making and hence not within one's ability to change. "I am old, retired, and alone" may be more a matter of circumstances imposed on the individual than a matter of free choice. Furthermore, a self-concept which took decades to construct may not readily adjust when confronted with dissonance resulting from circumstances not of one's own choosing. Where behaviors are difficult if not impossible to change, dissonance is not so easily resolved.

Another approach to alleviating dissonance involves adding behavioral elements which are more harmonious to the self-concept. Persons who think of themselves as helpers may find any number of ways in which to assist others—from holding a door open at the elevator to stuffing envelopes for the annual Red Cross drive. These and other additions have the effect of drowning out the dissonance and restoring consistency between behavior and self. If there is a disadvantage to this approach it may lie in its assumption of a high level of energy and a responsive environment, both of which could be problematic for many elderly persons.

A third alternative is to transform dissonance by reversing the negative evaluations. For example, the self-concept "I am old, retired, and alone" loses its demeaning qualities when society's general opinion becomes "It is *good* to be old, retired, and alone."

Finally, dissonance may also be disowned through a positive evaluation which simply ignores potentially negative behavior. This sort of dissonance reduction, in which past experience is presented as having been almost ideal, has been called halo reminiscence:

> A patient who was formerly a semiprofessional football player is contrasting the present-day player with those of his own day. "I remember the really great players who did everything well. The players nowadays fall asleep on the job. They're good players but there's something missing there. They seem to fall apart: don't have the spark; don't have the pep the old-time players used to have." It is striking that in his description of the present-day players, he attributes to them many of the symptoms of old age from which he himself suffers. This projection enables him to reinforce the denial of his own physical decline and identify himself more readily with the team representing the greater capacities of his youth. This halo effect is a conspicuous element in those reminiscences which depreciate the present and glorify the past. It is associated with the attitude that one has seen and been a part of the best and has nothing to regret.*

Life Review

Life review has been described as a universal mental process stimulated by "the realization of approaching dissolution and death. It marks the lives of all older persons in some manner as their myths of invulnerability or immortality give way"† and death becomes an approaching personal reality. The aged person looks back over life and tries to reconstruct, resolve, or otherwise reintegrate for one last time those things which have been most troublesome over the life-span. Such review need not be debilitating. Indeed experienced geriatric psychotherapists have pretty much laid to rest the old myths about the fragility of emotional health in normal elderly people. Robert N. Butler even describes the aged as "master survivors compared with the young. They can hardly be seen as inexperienced in defending themselves from the painful forces of life."*

Clinical experience has demonstrated that to care effectively for persons engaged in life review sensitive, respectful people do not need years of advanced training. The most needed skills are simply an ability to listen empathically and the capacity to let other persons experience again their own issues, without protectively trying to cover up pain and disappointment when these are the appropriate emotions. Writing in the preface of *All God's Dangers,* Theodore Rosengarten describes the effect reminiscing had on Nate Shaw, the ancient storyteller whose life and times have now been preserved for future generations:

> As our talks drew to a close the sessions grew longer. The initiative was his. Our work strengthened him and sustained his belief that his struggles had been worth the effort, although he had only recollections to show for them. These filled his days with a reality more powerful than the present.†

To be effective and helpful life review does not require a minute recounting of every significant event in obsessive chronological detail. What is significant is how the person resolves the old issues of life—resentment, dependence, love, bitterness, ambition, trust. Such a process can take place over an extended period of time, at a pace comfortable to the reminiscer, and can be as spontaneous and unrehearsed as a sandlot baseball game.

Neither is it necessary to think of life review as a heavy trip in psychotherapy. A reunion at a rural church (called Decoration Day in my childhood) in which people return from great distances to see friends and relatives, and place flowers on the graves of loved ones, can be as helpful as many structured therapy sessions.

Ministers are in a unique position to facilitate such activities in the context of a caring community. All it takes is imagination and the desire to get people together. At your next potluck supper try having people of various ages seated at one table—according to the month of their birthdays. All the Februaries sit together at one table and all the Junes at another. I guarantee you there will be an intergenerational age spread and some good fun. Or at your next mother-daughter luncheon get the moms to bring their old schooldays scrapbooks or old photographs (they might even need to write or visit *their* moms to get them!) and share them with their daughters, who have also brought their own scrapbooks. In various ways the church can facilitate life review. Reminiscence can involve just you and one other person. It can also take place in small groups of elderly people or it can be intergenerational. A whole series of small group meetings might be devoted to sharing summations of the participants' lifework, with special emphasis on how things have changed over the years. Imagine a carpenter spending most of one session talking about how electricity and power tools have changed his work and modified the techniques of construction, or a physician remarking at length about how his older colleagues responded when he moved into a rural community with a "new-fangled invention" called the microscope.

Facilitating Reminiscence

The chart here included is based on personal experiences and the experiences of others known to me. I hope it will remind you of significant events from your own life and at the same time inspire your imagination with respect to the possibilities inherent in your situation. It may help you think about ways in which various activities could be structured to accentuate the recreational or therapeutic qualities of reminiscence, or to encourage interpersonal relationships and enhance intimacy. Use your own insights and creativity to develop some specific ideas and programs for your particular setting.

Autobiography

A small, portable tape recorder can help appreciably in the pastoral use of reminiscence, especially for persons whose eyesight is deteriorating or who can no longer write legibly. A recorded autobiography can communicate so much more than the written word: inflection, tone, emphasis, pronunciation are all captured for posterity. Recordings can also be saved for the use of the great-grandchildren when they become old enough to appreciate family history.

POLAR QUALITIES

FACILITATIVE ACTIVITIES	*Therapeutic*	*Recreational*	*Interpersonal*	*Solitary*	*Distancing*	*Enhances Intimacy*
Autobio-graphies	x	x	x	x	x	x
Reunions	x	x	x			x
Genealogies		x		x	x	
Pilgrimages	x		x	x		x
Scrapbooks, Photo Albums	x	x	x	x		x
Lifework Summations	x		x			x
Oral Family Histories	x		x			x
Oral Local Church Histories	x	x	x			x

Imagine that you, a middle-aged American touring Europe, are standing on a street in a Czechoslovakian town. As you look down the road you turn on your tape recorder and the voice of your late great-grandmother comes alive. Words and accents which you barely remember from childhood come flooding back to you as your glance takes in the simple cemetery holding the grave of a frightened young girl's mother, who died 120 years ago:

> I was experiencing deep, conflicting emotions as I stood there waiting for the train. It was a very difficult situation for a sixteen-year-old girl.
> I was waiting for the train in my home village of Zbecno, Bohemia, for the start of the trip to my new home in America. That was June 15, 1903, I shall never forget that date.
> Of course I was excited and thrilled and enthused to be going to the United States—and rather naturally a little nervous.
> But I also was very sad. My four sisters and little brother were there to tell me good-bye; all crying. My many friends from the little village where I had grown up, came to tell me goodbye—and

brush away the tears. They knew, and I knew, that I never would see them again.

I looked down the street several blocks to the cemetery, with the white stone fence, where my mother was buried. She died when I was eleven years old.

My older sister, who had looked after me and the other small children after my mother's death, was there. Yes, yes there were truly mixed emotions that June 15th, and most of them sad. I have never forgotten them, even though it was seventy-four years ago and the United States has given me wonderful advantages and a fine family, well educated.*

Pilgrimage

Journeys to significant places can be an important means of helping older people review the past. A particularly successful pilgrimage would combine at least two generations. The older person would be able to share the memories evoked, while the younger person would gain additional insight into himself through such participation in his family's past. When I was a college student my grandmother and I went to visit the site of her old village community. The memories of this visit are still fresh and meaningful:

Before the turn of the century the village had been a thriving little community with several stores and small shops. I could even imagine how the main street might have looked nestled down there among the large shade trees. There's hardly anything left now besides this row of trees—plus a few bricks near the spring, where the old post office stood for years after everything else was gone. It was the county seat back then. Can you believe that—a courthouse and everything?

> *Granny, how does it feel to come back after so long and find that nothing much is left?*

We climb the hill to the simple old frame church, the only building still in use. Outside, from beneath the shade trees, it looks plain, even ascetic, yet sort of peaceful and sturdy. Inside, the benches are smooth and invite you to run your hands over them. No electricity. Hymn books published fifty years ago. A potbellied stove. This communion rail saw a lot of weddings, baptisms, and funerals in its day, not to forget the revival conversions and the anguished prayers of persons kneeling alone during the week. About to leave, I notice the old loft where the Masonic lodge used to meet, with only wasps flying lazily back and forth at the door. Everything is so quiet and serene.

>*Granny, do you remember the Sundays when it was filled with people?*

>*Why am I here anyway?*

>*The boys at the fraternity house just wouldn't understand.*
>*Maybe they already know who they are.*
>*I couldn't imagine one of them standing here with his Granny, like me.*

The cemetery is the key. It just has to be really old because it is so big, with those funny flat tombstones for the people born in Culpeper County, Virginia and Edgefield County, South Carolina. Names like Henry and Coker and Morris and Christian are everywhere. Oh, and look at all the little graves! Every family has at least one of the small ones.

>*Granny, can you tell me who I am?*

Come here son and look at this!
Tommy Sutton rests here.
He lived at the farm next to ours.
Must've died when we were eight years old.
Lordy, a lot of people were sick that summer!
Tommy had pretty blond hair and big freckles.
We used to tease him about a crooked toe the horse stepped on.

This is where my Uncle Silas is buried.

>*Who's that, Granny?*

Silas?
Why Silas was my favorite.
He even took me and Page to Montgomery once.
Bought me the prettiest dress you ever did see.
Red polka dots.
You can see them on the quilt in the back room still.
I'd forgotten Uncle Silas gave me that dress though. . . .
He was a big man.
Tall and handsome.
Wore a full beard.
Was always full of mischief.

Why here's Bertha Coggon's grave!
Everybody called her Aunt Bertha.
Always had something sweet for us kids to eat.
She must've weighed two hundred pounds.
Had the happiest laugh.
I remember the night of the fire, how Pop went galloping off when

he saw the smoke, and came home all red-eyed and quiet, smelling
like a fireplace.
Us kids thought he'd been crying or something.

Slowly we stroll through the cemetery. Names I could vaguely
remember hearing as a child pop up out of the ground on marble
complete with a story. I laugh a lot, even cry once or twice.
It is still powerful stuff.

Oral History

In recent years oral history has become very popular among
serious historians. It is also as an effective method of teaching
history to young people. The idea can be used effectively in a
church or family setting with or without a tape recorder.

Imagine the possibilities for a family night workshop where the
goal is to develop scenes significant in the history of each family.
Only those events which are directly remembered could be used.
Each participant would decide which personal memory is worthy
and share it with the family group, who could then ask questions
or add details from their own memories. The generations could be
talking and listening to each other with a renewed appreciation
for a shared history. Painful events as well as funny stories might
all be a part of the total experience.

Memorable scenes exist within every family, needing only an
opportunity to surface. The following vignette is a delightful
reminiscence from childhood by Kenneth R. Mitchell, Dean at
Dubuque Theological Seminary. Younger generations in any
family might well sing the hymn "Come Ye Thankful People"
with new appreciation if they had shared in this event at a family
workshop. Think of the possibilities.

"Play Smut?"
She is eighty-five now; I am twelve. Harder to talk to her, easy
to listen. If I play the silly game she may tell stories.
"OK."
"I'll sit here on the couch. You get the cards."
"Here they are. I'll deal. Aunt Laura, what was Harvest
Home?"
"What do you want to know for?" Not suspicious, just in-
trigued that I should ask.
"I thought of it when we were singing 'Come Ye Thankful
People' at church."
"Well, it was like a fair, and then again it wasn't. They had it

over in Westwood, you know. There was a park there just for Harvest Home."

"Did they have rides? Fours and tens."

"Oh no, nothing like that. Kings."

"Jacks and eights. Well, what was it for?"

"Elevens. Say, these are your Aunt Florence's Five Hundred cards."

"That's OK; they work the same way. Fives. What was Harvest Home for?"

"Nines and twelves. Aces. Why, people brought their harvest samples: corn and hogs and everything."

"Did they have prizes like the fair? Sixes."

"Eights. Yes, and I suppose that's what some people came for."

"Not everybody?"

"Well, the original idea was to thank the Lord for a good harvest. Deuces. I'm out and you're smutted."

"And that's what people went for, really?"

"Some of them. Are these my cards?"

"Yes. What about the others?"

"Treys and fives. Why, that was where people went courting. Jessie—your grandmother—met your grandfather there. Sister Ella met her husband there too. What've you got?"

"Fours and elevens. What do you mean, courting?"

"Nines. Courting means talking, but if it doesn't get beyond talking it isn't courting."

"Tens and queens. I don't understand."

"Well, I'm not married so I guess I didn't understand either. Ha. I'm out and you're smutted."*

5. Completing the Task

> The church of Jesus Christ ought to know something about libera-
> tion and the gospel, and it ought to know something about com-
> munity from the Old and New Testaments. It has the opportunity
> in this new age to be a truly liberating force.*
>
> —Maggie Kuhn

In a small book such as this only a few ideas can be discussed and
a few examples given. The most important chapter is still yours to
write.

Narrowing the Focus

Within your particular context of ministry perhaps this final
chapter should be on the meaning and significance of *home* for
the elderly's sense of well-being. For the aged particularly a
home is not just a place where one eats and sleeps; frequently it is
also the locus of one's identity, a collage of all the sacrifices
made in behalf of autonomy and independence down through the
years. To live among familiar surroundings can even be a survival issue for some people.

Yet home is not necessarily restricted to an individual resi-
dence or apartment, nor does it exclude an institutional setting or
three-generation family. A sense of home involves security, con-
tinuity, and an atmosphere which maximizes personal responsibility and realistic autonomy without attaching negative connota-
tions to the acceptance of help in the furtherance of these goals.

In many communities the aged person faces an unhappy choice
between complete personal independence and institutional care,
neither of which is exactly appropriate to actual needs. Sometimes the central need—for groceries or even for a medical
regimen—can be met by volunteers on a regular basis in the
person's own home. In some communities local churches and
synagogues have been successful in developing an enabling

ministry to accomplish this goal. Perhaps a beginning point for you would be to learn more about such a program through contacting The Shepherds' Center,* which has utilized elderly persons as volunteers actively reaching out to other elderly persons.

Perhaps for your ministry the concluding chapter of this book should instead be about the significant role churches can play in retirement and preretirement planning, or about continuing education in the sixties and beyond, or even about the possibilities of lay ministry for elderly persons. The list of potential topics is considerable. The point is that you alone have the insight to write a concluding chapter which is relevant to your locus of ministry.

Take a few minutes to jot down some of the unmet needs in your community or congregation. Then list the resources and strengths available in your setting. Notice any discrepancies between the two lists and consider whether the experience of ministers elsewhere may potentially be of help to you in meeting certain needs. Specify what you would like to find out in regard to needs and resources in your community and elsewhere as they may relate to your ideas for ministry.

In Appendix B I have described a select number of organizations and sources of information. With your list of questions at hand see if it suggests resources and ideas which look promising to you for your ministry of care and counseling. Sometimes aged individuals or families struggling with problems involving an aged member might wish additional information about available services of which they are unaware, for example, alternatives to institutional care, or rehabilitation programs. Would it be helpful for them to read something about what to expect of the aged? What guidelines can be used to "grade" a nursing home? The Annotated Bibliography may be of further help to you in such situations.

Charting a Course

There are many ways in which you and your church may decide to work with the aged in your community. You may want to sponsor a group and help it join a national organization for the aged, or just provide an existent group with encouragement and a place for meeting. Some type of transportation program may be needed for church and community activities. If education is your specialty you may want to provide short-term or even long-term courses of particular interest to the aging, possibly even as part of church school. Churches often sponsor preschools and kindergartens—why not an educational experience for adults? Or your church may decide to become involved with other groups in providing needed services to the aged on a community level. Successful programs in various parts of the country range from Meals on Wheels to household help to craft shows. All such programs might best be self-directed by the aged themselves particularly if the talent is available.

As we learn to value persons across the entire life-span we may begin to actualize the wholeness God has intended for us. A major task for us as individuals and as persons in leadership roles is to become more whole within ourselves. Where the healing process begins within we will reach out to life and encourage others to join us in this growth.

I believe that you, as a person concerned about aging and ministry, are part of a creative movement whose boundaries expand with each new experimental development in the local church's ministry with aging people. As yet the horizon is not even in sight. The need for your creativity and service is enormous. This small book must end, but your chapter has yet to be written, for only you can do what now needs to be done.

Appendix A
Images and Expectations

Self-Image and Public Image of Older Persons

Very friendly and warm

Very wise from experience

Very bright and alert

Very open-minded and adaptable

Very good at getting things done

Very active physically

Very active sexually

■ Self-image of public 65 and older

▨ Total public image of "most people over 65"

0 10 20 30 40 50 60 70 80 90 100

Percent

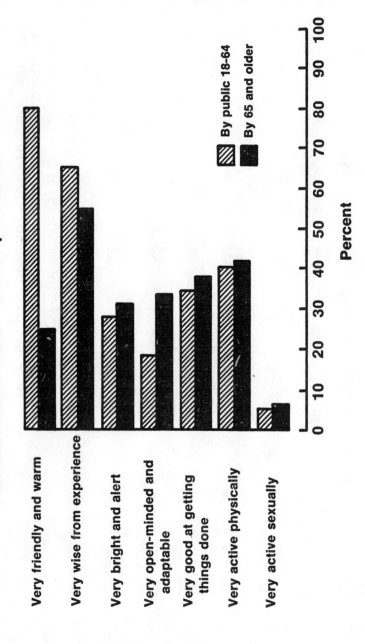

Qualities Attributed to "Most People Over 65"

By public 18-64

By 65 and older

Very friendly and warm

Very wise from experience

Very bright and alert

Very open-minded and adaptable

Very good at getting things done

Very active physically

Very active sexually

Percent

Personal Experience vs. Public Expectation Regarding Problems of Age

	Percentage of public '65 and older personally experiencing problem as "very" or "somewhat" serious	Percentage of total public attributing problem as "very" serious for most people over 65	Net Difference
Poor health	50	51	+1
Fear of crime	47	50	+3
Not having enough money to live on	40	62	+22
Loneliness	29	60	+31
Not enough education	25	20	-5
Not enough medical care	23	44	+21
Not feeling needed	19	50	+31
Not enough to do to keep busy	17	37	+20
Not enough friends	16	28	+12
Not enough job opportunities	12	45	+33
Poor housing	11	35	+24
Not enough clothing	8	16	+8

"A Lot of Time" Spent by Older People in Various Activities

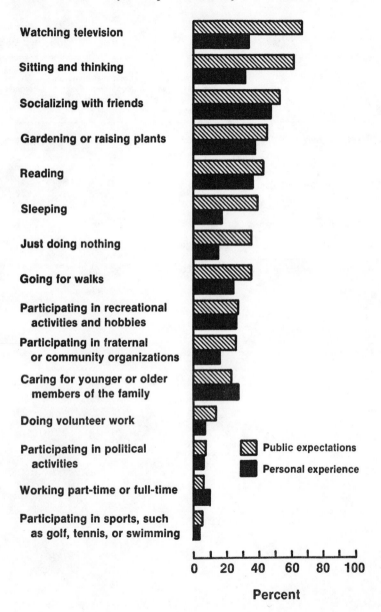

Appendix B
Where You Can Find Out

For convenience this list of potentially helpful resources is divided into five sections: organizations to which the aged themselves belong; organizations (including religious and civic groups) providing services and programs not limited to age; organizations of groups providing services or care; organizations of experts on aging; and organizations providing primarily information. The attached information concerning each has been derived mainly from the organizations' own printed materials, many of which offer rich possibilities for creative adaptation to new situations.

Groups for the Aged

Gray Panthers
3700 Chestnut Street
Philadelphia, Pennsylvania 19104

This action-oriented group of old and young is "committed to the creation of a society where all people are able to fulfill their highest potential and where there is recognition of both the value and needs of every human being." Since its founding in 1970 the movement has concentrated on the problems of ageism (age discrimination and age stereotyping), dealing with such significant issues as compulsory retirement, the health crisis, housing, inflation, hunger, and nursing home reform. A national newspaper, the Gray Panther *Network*, is published several times a year in large-type format.

Institute for Retired Professionals
New School for Social Research
66 West 12th Street
New York, New York 10011

The Institute was begun in 1962 as a program developed by retirees with the help and encouragement of the New School. The first educational venture of its kind in the United States, it has since influenced the development of similar

71

programs at other universities (for example, the University of California at San Francisco and at San Diego, and Case Western Reserve University). It offers highly trained professionals the opportunity in retirement to renew their education at the university level without usual course procedures. This self-directed program is unique in adult education: both the students and the teachers are retirees. For example, retired journalists, writers, editors, and advertising executives publish the *IRP Review*. Opportunities for socializing and for community service are also provided. While this particular program is limited to New York City, its curriculum guide and other information would be of interest to anyone concerned with educational programs for older adults.

International Senior Citizen Association, Inc.
11753 Wilshire Boulevard
Los Angeles, California 90025

ISCA is an independent nonpartisan, nonprofit organization open to all older individuals and groups of older people. Founded in 1963 in Copenhagen, Denmark, it seeks to establish communication between older persons for educational and cultural development, and to cooperate with nonprofit and government agencies "working for the welfare and happiness of older people throughout the world." For its members and affiliates from many nations ISCA publishes the *International Senior Citizens News*.

National Association of Retired Federal Employees
1533 New Hampshire Avenue, N.W.
Washington, D.C. 20036

Since 1921 NARFE has served as spokesman for retired Federal employees and their survivors. It has been the major advocate for updating and liberalizing the Civil Service Retirement Law. The organization endorses a broad range of health, life, auto, and homeowners and tenants insurance plans plus a mail-order drug service and a travel service. It publishes the monthly magazine *Retirement Life*, as well as helpful materials about legal aspects of planning—wills, insurance, financial obligations, funerals—much of which is applicable to the retired and the preretired generally.

National Council of Senior Citizens, Inc.
1511 K Street, N.W.
Washington, D.C. 20005

This nonpartisan, nonprofit organization is "committed to winning a better life for older Americans." The largest organization of older people's clubs in the nation, it provides several service programs to members—low-cost drugs, travel, health protection supplemental to Medicare—and seeks to involve senior citizens personally in social and political action on federal, state, and community levels. The Council publishes monthly *The Senior Citizen News*. A number of unions affiliated with the AFL-CIO urge their retiring members to join NCSC.

National Federation of Grandmother Clubs of America
Suite 1302
203 North Wabash Avenue
Chicago, Illinois 60601

This nonsectarian, nonpartisan, nonprofit organization founded in 1938 for women who are grandmothers now has approximately eighteen thousand members. Local clubs, easily formed, exist primarily to further the social and educational interests of the members. Benevolent projects contribute to research on children's diseases. The national quarterly is *Autumn Leaves*.

National Retired Teachers Association
and
American Association of Retired Persons
1909 K Street, N.W.
Washington, D.C. 20049

These two large and outstanding organizations for retired persons share founders, headquarters, and many programs and services. Members' benefits include a travel service, courtesy discounts, vacation holidays, group health insurance, and mail-order pharmacy service. NRTA/AARP also offer an exceptional array of community service programs both on the national level and through local chapters, including materials and/or complete courses in consumer protection, crime prevention, driver improvement, health education (Vigor in Maturity, or VIM), housing, senior community service aides, widowed persons service, tax aides, and the Institute of Lifetime Learning. The church relations program provides assistance in developing outreach programs, retirement planning programs, spiritual counseling, and elderly involvement in church-sponsored recreation activities and community service activities. AARP also sponsors a Generations Allied Program (GAP) aimed at breaking age barriers to communication and friendship. The Action for Independent Maturity (AIM) division of AARP emphasizes preretirement planning. Both NRTA and AARP publish monthly magazines and news bulletins.

Organizations Not Limited by Age

B'nai B'rith
1640 Rhode Island Avenue, N.W.
Washington, D.C. 20036

But for What? the B'nai B'rith Community Volunteers Services publication, provides a good guide to programs which can enhance the lives of older adults who suffer from poverty, ill-health, loneliness and isolation, and inadequate housing. It has a section on the aged volunteer and methods of combating the problem of inactivity. The Commission on Community and Veterans Services' program called Reach out . . . and touch! is designed to bring a touch of Jewish life to older people (and others) living in isolation from a Jewish community; many aspects of the program can, of course, be applied to any religion.

Kiwanis International
101 East Erie Street
Chicago, Illinois 60611

The Greater Years, a project guide for Kiwanis Clubs serving the aging, contains suggestions for determining needs and for planning and implementing a variety of services including Senior Volunteers, arts, meals programs, transportation services, health screening, discounts, education and library services, manpower and gardening services, information and referral centers, film programs and special events, and church-related services. Kiwanis also makes available a fine seminar program on "Preparation for Retirement" developed by The National Council on Aging.

National Council of Jewish Women
1 West 47th Street
New York, New York 10036

In 1976 the NCJW published *Continuing Choices,* a significant idea and implementation handbook of programs designed to act as a stimulus for community planning of creative programs for and with the aging: standard programs such as meals and transportation, but also other programs involving legal services, oral history, sheltered workshops, craftsmen's exchanges, social action and advocacy, and widows' and widowers' consultation services.

United Auto Workers (Retired and Older Workers Department)
8731 East Jefferson
Detroit, Michigan 48214

Information provided by this outstanding program includes a number of preparation-for-retirement booklets developed by the Division of Gerontology of the University of Michigan and used in the preretirement programs of UAW and of the Chrysler Corporation. Guidelines for community services programs of UAW Retired Workers Chapters provide useful suggestions about getting involved. Schedules of activities at UAW Retired Workers Centers and brochures on "Travel Adventure" give some idea about activity-oriented possibilities. Pamphlets and bulletins provide useful information on common drugs, on condominiums, and on helping a couple plan the handling of practical matters at the death of a spouse.

Woman's Auxiliary to the American Medical Association
535 North Dearborn Street
Chicago, Illinois 60610

Its *Services to Aging Package Program* is a handy folder containing a wealth of vital information on services to the aging that any group can start: meals, homemaker-home health aide, telephone reassurance, escort, friendly visiting, congregate dining, senior centers, and handyman. The packet includes a brief summary of needs, methods, and resources; reports of successful projects; significant government documents about home accident prevention, telephone reassurance programs, and nutrition for the elderly; and a National Council on Aging Publication List.

Service and Care Groups

International Federation on Aging
1909 K Street, N.W., Room 616
Washington, D.C. 20049

The Federation was created in 1973 to bring together various national organizations that represent or provide services to the elderly, organizations whose goal is primarily that of improving the life of aging persons (NRTA/AARP are active members in the United States). A quarterly publication, *Aging International,* provides practitioners with cross-cultural information on program innovation and service delivery, practical applications of research results in social gerontology, and developments in aging policy within international and regional organizations (United Nations, World Health Organization, Council of Europe). *Home Help Services for the Aging Around the World* is a recent publication on a single issue.

National Council for Homemaker-Home Health Aide Services, Inc.
67 Irving Place
New York, New York 10003

This national standard-setting organization provides supervision and accreditation for local homemaker-home health services of the kind that can sometimes enable aging individuals to maintain themselves in their own homes. The National Council provides advice and information on effective community support for already-existing programs and on development of a local service.

National Council of Health Care Services
1200 15th Street, N.W., Suite 402
Washington, D.C. 20005

Founded in 1969, the Council is a group of tax-paying health care companies owning and/or managing nursing homes, hospitals, psychiatric facilities, clinics, pharmacies, home health agencies, surgical supply companies, homemaker services, and child day care centers. Its primary goal is the delivery of quality health care at a reasonable cost.

Urban Elderly Coalition
Alice M. Brophy, Chairman
Mayor's Office for the Aging
250 Broadway
New York, New York 10007

This national association brings together municipal executives on aging from a number of the nation's largest cities to share information and to write on behalf of the twelve million older people who live in urban centers. The Coalition meets with federal officials such as the United States Commissioner on Aging and the United States Senate Select Committee on Aging. Associate membership is open to interested individuals and groups.

Experts on Aging

American Aging Association (AGE)
c/o Denham Harman, M.D., Executive Director
University of Nebraska Medical Center
Omaha, Nebraska 68105

AGE is a relatively new national lay-scientific health organization patterned after the American Heart Association. It was formed to meet the pressing need for more biomedical research on aging, and with a view to finding ways of increasing functional life-span. It publishes *AGE News* periodically.

The Gerontology Society
1 Dupont Circle, Suite 520
Washington, D.C. 20036

This is the national organization for professional educators and researchers in the various fields of aging. The Society seeks to promote the scientific study of aging, to stimulate communications between disciplines, to broaden education in aging, and to foster practical applications of research. Issues of its *Journal of Gerontology* and *The Gerontologist,* each published six times per year, usually contain information of interest to nonspecialists and occasionally to religious workers.

National Caucus on the Black Aged
The National Center on Black Aged
1730 M Street, N.W., Suite 811
Washington, D.C. 20036

Founded in 1970 by a number of experts in the field of aging, this organization attempts to recognize the unique problems of the black aged and to develop programs specifically tailored to them in such areas as income, housing, and health services.

The National Council on the Aging, Inc.
1828 L Street, N.W.
Washington, D.C. 20036

The NCOA is not a direct service agency but a resource for professionals working with older people. Founded by a group of people in social welfare, virtually every facet of the field of aging has been or is a component of its programs. NCOA works with national voluntary agencies, with local, state, and federal agencies, with the private sector, and with the academic world. It sponsors numerous publications. Special interests include the National Institute of Industrial Gerontology, the National Institute of Senior Centers, and community organizations and development.

Information Sources

Consultation on Programs for the Aging
Family Service Association of America
44 East 23rd Street
New York, New York 10010

The Association is a social work organization which provides information on the aged primarily for social workers. The books, pamphlets, and articles from the FSAA journal *Social Casework,* gathered together by the Consultation, are valuable for anyone who works with the aged. An annotated bibliography on the aging is especially helpful with respect to the aging process and behavior characteristics of the aged.

Sex Information and Education Council of the United States
122 East 42nd Street, Suite 922
New York, New York 10017

SIECUS is a national voluntary health organization concerned with human sexuality throughout the life cycle. It believes that "aging people are too often deprived of opportunities for sexual companionship and expression, which they need despite unscientific belief to the contrary. Society has an obligation to create conditions conducive to the fulfillment of these needs." It serves as a clearinghouse for information on available printed and audio-visual materials, a programming consultant, and a creator of original books, study guides, and bibliographies, certain of which are relevant for those interested in the aged.

National Easter Seal Society for Crippled Children and Adults
2023 West Ogden Avenue
Chicago, Illinois 60612

The goal of the Society has always been "to improve the quality of life for the disabled and the handicapped." The oldest and largest voluntary health agency serving the handicapped, it has a nationwide program of treatment, research, and education. Advocacy on both the local and the national level has recently become a major concern of the Easter Seal societies. The National Society has available a number of publications useful to the disabled aged and those who work or live with them, for example, on how to organize a stroke club for stroke patients and their families.

Notes

Page

2. * Robert Browning, *Poetical Works, 1833–1864*, ed. Ian Jac (London: Oxford University Press, 1970), pp. 811–18.
5. * Ecclesiastes 12:1–7 (JB).
7. * Seward Hiltner, "Facts and Needs: Present and Future," in *Toward a Theology of Aging*, ed. Seward Hiltner (New York: Human Sciences Press, 1975), p. 97.
9. * Adapted from Betsie Carter, "The Door," *Synthesis* 1(1):WB50, 1974.
14. * Louis Harris and Associates, Inc., *The Myth and Reality of Aging in America* (Washington: National Council on Aging, Inc., 1976).
19. * Paul W. Pruyser, "Aging: Downward, Upward, or Forward?" in *Toward a Theology of Aging*, ed. Seward Hiltner (New York: Human Sciences Press, 1975), p. 103.
19. † John B. Cobb, Jr., *Theology and Pastoral Care* (Philadelphia: Fortress Press, 1977), p. 11.
24. * Ibid., p. 52.
24. † Ibid., p. 51.
25. * Roberto Assagioli, *Psychosynthesis: A Manual of Principles and Techniques* (New York: Hobbs, Dorman & Company, Inc., 1965), p. 280.
25. † Ibid., p. 18.
26. * Ibid., p. 87.
26. † Graham Taylor, "The Verbal 'Who Am I?' Technique in Psychotherapy," in *Approaches to the Self: The "Who Am I?" Techniques in Psychotherapy*, P.R.F. Issue No. 23 (New York: Psychosynthesis Research Foundation, 1968), pp. 12–13; italics mine.
26. ‡ Ibid., p. 17.
31. * Celia Dale, "The Very End of Summer," *Women's Day*, 23 August 1977, pp. 74, 198.
31. † Robert C. Peck, "Psychological Developments in the Second Half of Life," in *Middle Age and Aging*, ed. Bernice L. Neugarten (Chicago: University of Chicago Press, 1968), p. 89.
40. * Ann Landers, "Ann Landers," *Des Moines Register*, 18 June 1977. Reprinted by permission of Field Newspaper Syndicate.
42. * Simone de Beauvoir, *A Very Easy Death*, trans. Patrick O'Brian (New York: Warner Books, 1973), p. 123.
52. * Allen Pincus, "Reminiscence in Aging and Its Implications for Social Work Practice," *Social Work* 15 (July 1970): 51.

53. * Charles N. Lewis, "The Adaptive Value of Reminiscing in Old Age," *Journal of Geriatric Psychology* 6 (1973): 119.
54. * Arthur W. McMahon and Paul J. Rhudick, "Reminiscing," *Archives of General Psychiatry* 10 (1964): 295.
54. ✝ Myrna Lewis and Robert N. Butler, "Life Review Therapy: Putting Memories to Work in Individual and Group Psychotherapy," *Geriatrics*, November 1974, p. 165.
55. * Ibid., p. 169.
55. ✝ Theodore Rosengarten, *All God's Dangers: The Life of Nate Shaw* (New York: Avon Books, 1974), p. xx.
58. * Barbara Soucek to Irving B. Weber, "Barbara Soucek Remembers Leaving Homeland 74 Years Ago," *Iowa City Press-Citizen*, 3 August 1977.
61. * Kenneth R. Mitchell, "I'm Out and You're Smutted," from an unpublished article.
63. * Charley Lerrigo, "Are Old People the Champions of New Ideas?" *United Methodist Women*, September 1976, p. 29. An interview with Maggie Kuhn, National Convener of the Gray Panthers.
64. * The Shepherds' Center, 5218 Oak Street, Kansas City, Missouri, 64112.

Annotated Bibliography

Arnold, Oren. *Guide Yourself Through Old Age*. Philadelphia: Fortress Press, 1976. A breezy popular primer that can be put in the hands of the nonprofessional.

Atcheley, Robert C. *The Social Forces in Later Life*. 2nd ed. Belmont, California: Wadsworth Publishing Company, Inc., 1977. A good technical look at those factors which shape aging in America.

Buckley, Joseph C., and Schmidt, Henry. *The Retirement Handbook: A Complete Planning Guide to Your Future*. 4th ed. New York: Harper and Row, 1971. Start planning your church retirement program by reading this book.

Butler, Robert N. *Why Survive?: Being Old in America*. New York: Harper and Row, 1975. Your task force on aging needs to digest this 470 page polemic—get it for *them*, then read it yourself.

Butler, Robert N., and Lewis, Myrna I. *Aging and Mental Health: Positive Psychosocial Approaches*. St. Louis: The C. V. Mosby Company, 1973. Written for health professionals, but full of implications for ministry.

———. *Sex After Sixty: A Guide for Men and Women for Their Later Years*. New York: Harper and Row, 1976. After you read this book, place it on your shelf in plain view.

Hiltner, Seward, ed. *Toward a Theology of Aging*. New York: Human Sciences Press, 1975. Stimulating reflection on theological and philosophical issues in aging.

Hoyt, Murray. *Creative Retirement: Planning the Best Years Yet*. Charlotte, Vermont: Garden Way Publishing, 1974. A chatty, helpful look at some styles of retirement.

Kalish, Richard A. *Late Adulthood: Perspectives on Human Development*. Belmont, California: Brooks/Cole Publishing Company, 1975. Readable presentation of basic psychological and psychosocial data.

Neugarten, Bernice L., ed. *Middle Age and Aging: A Reader in Social Psychology*. Chicago: University of Chicago Press, 1968. A valuable collection of essays for persons who want to read only one book.

Nouwen, Henri J.M., and Gaffney, Walter J. *Aging: The Fulfillment of Life*. Garden City, New York: Image Books, 1976. A sensitive, poetic expression of aging and ministry.

Rosengarten, Theodore. *All God's Dangers: The Life of Nate Shaw*. New York: Alfred A. Knopf, Inc., 1974. This oral history of an illiterate black man is one of the most powerful examples I know of life review reminiscence.

Stenger, Wallace. *The Spectator Bird*. Garden City, New York: Doubleday and Company, Inc., 1976. Not many novels are told from the point of view of a seventy-year-old. This one details a therapeutic experience of shared reminiscence, as well as day-to-day coping with being old.